Whistler Weekend Cookbook

Easy, Elegant Recipes by local Chefs & Friends

by Elsie Cumming

Front Cover:
Chateau Whistler Resort
with Executive Chef
Bernard Casavant

Photographed by:
Mark van Maneau
Vancouver Sun

Bernard Casavant

Bernard Casavant, Executive Chef, of the Chateau Whistler Resort has been selected by the National Culinary committee to be the sole Canadian representative of the Bocuse D'or International Competition to be held in Lyon, France on January 22 and 23, 1991.

Born and raised in Port Alberni, Bernard graduated from Malaspina College in 1976. He is a member of the B.C. Chef's Association, and has successfully completed the CFCC Chef de Cuisine Certification program.

Bernard's background history includes the Canadian Club where he worked as Executive Chef for Expo '86; The Wedgewood Hotel, as Executive Chef; Delta Mountain Inn, Executive Chef; Four Season Hotel, as Executive Sous Chef; and Canadian Pacific's Chateau Whistler Resort, as Executive Chef. Bernard was appointed Executive Chef at the Chateau in July, 1989 prior to the Grand opening in November 1989.

Restaurants

Ambrosia	938-1921
Araxi's Restaurant & Bar	R.932-4540
Baker's Cottage	932-2235
Border Cantina	932-3373
Chez Joël	R.932-2112
Citta's	932-4177
Florentynas	R.932-4424
Il Caminetto di Umberto	R.932-4442
Keg at the Mountain	932-5151
Les Deux Gros Restaurante	932-4611
The Longhorn	932-5999
La Fiesta - The Hot Rock Cafe	938-2040
Lu Garden	R.932-6431
Maddison's	932-6666
Original Ristorante	932-6408
Peter's Underground	932-4811
Planter's Restaurant	R.932-1133
Rim Rock Cafe & Oyster Bar	R.932-5565
Sushi Village	R.932-3330
Tapley's Pub	932-4011
Teppan Village	932-2223
Trattoria Umberto	932-5858
Twiggs Restaurant & Lounge	932-1982
Wildflower Cafe	938-2033

Contents

Breakfast & Brunch

Mid-day & Apre Ski or...

Southside Hot Antipasto Hero   20
Cream of Ginger Carrot Soup   21
The Hot Gourmet   22

Appetizers & First Courses

Shrimp Gazpacho Avaxi   23
Smoked Oysters in Soyo Sauce   24
Greek Stuffed Cherry Tomatoes   24
Cantina Wings Con Pina   25
Avaxi's Creamy Vinaigrette & Greens   26
Indonesian Peanut Sauce & Vegatables 27
Honey & Garlic Prawns   28
Made in Greece Satziki   29
Priscilla's Artichoke Dip   30
Liz' Crab Dip   30
Artichoke Amour   31
Acapulco North Ceviche   32
Asparagus Mousse   33
Pika Seafood in Puff Pastry   34
Roast Carrot & Brie Soup   35
Shitake & Scallops   36
Mulligatawny Soup   37

The Main Event

Moules Mariniere	39
Jean Pierre's Sole Pecheur	40
Lousiana North Barbecued Shrimp	41
Jansson's Frestelse / Swedish Potatoes	42
Ty's Saskatchewan Lobster	43
Lu Garden Black Pepper Steak	44
Chicken Breasts with Watercress & Ginger	45
Don's Squash & Cheddar Casserole	46
Escalopes of Salmon	47
Beef Bourguignon René	48
Fettucine with Asparagus	49
Coriander, Cornmeal Crusted Boston Blue	50
Fettucine with Clam & Basil Sauce	52
Michael's Gone Fishing Ginger Salmon	53
Mountain Stream Trout with Orange & Tarragon	54
Orange & Tarragon Sauce	55
Isabelle's Beef Dijon	56
Ambrosia Chicken Oscar	57
Pheasant with Mountain Blueberries	59
Tempura Toshi	60
Marinated Artichokes, Proscuitto Ham ...	62
Black Forest Chicken-Hunter Style	64
Montreal West Tortiere	65
Wild Flower Vinegar	66

cont.

Cheese Fondue Savoyarde	68
Salmon Tarragon	70
Tired of Turkey Pie	71
Daves Creekhouse Chops	72
Enchiladas Del-Norta	73
Currey Prawns with Coconut	74
Sea to Sky Seafood Lasagne	75
Renée's Luxembourg Sweet Purple Cabbage	76
Luxembourg Potato Pancakes	76
Pork with Avgolemono Sauce	77
Chicken with Mustard & Lemon Sauce	78
Mahi Mahi with Bourbon Pecan Cream	79
Chicken Floventyna	80
Russel's Brussels	81

Desserts

Schwarzwald Torte	82
Okanagon Pears in Red Wine	83
Doug's Pumpkin Cheese cake	84
Alta Vista Chalet Apricot Torte	85
Banana's Flambé & Ice Cream	86
Snow Angel's Pie	87
Frozen Nouget, Frangelico Parfait	88
Cheesecake with fresh fruit	90

cont.

Easy St. Chocolate Rum Mousse	91
Mountain Blueberries & Zabaglion	92
Bakers Cottage Chocolate Pecan Pie	93
Orange Tofu Mousse	94
White & Dark Chocolate Mousse Pie	95
Alsation Pears	96
Molly's Sunshine Pie	97
Citta's Pecan Pie	98

Warmers & Coolers

Citta Coffee	99
Hoz's Coffee	99
Longhorn Royal Flush	99
Parker's Paralizer	100
Tommy Africa's Martini	100
Barts Place Bamm Bamm	101
Black Forest Coffee	101
Latte Chez Joël	101
Café Latte Joël	102
Tapley's Junior	102
Rim Rock Roll.	102
Han's & Andi's Red Balloon	103
Raspberry Desire	103
Barry T.'s Big O!	103

Cont.

Club 10 Tony's 10 Dream	104
Florentyna's Licorice Nut	104
Planters Lounge Highland Martini	104
Cuz's Strawberry Melon Marquirita	105
Banana Nectar	105
Barry T.'s Shannon Shooter	105
Rum Cream Liqueur	106
Coffee & Vanilla Liqueur	106

Goodies & Supplies for your pack etc.

Chocolate Chip Cookie Chalet	107
Herschell's Favorite Carrot Cake	109
Olga's Cream Cheese Icing	110
Whistler Valley Trail Mix	110
Skiier's Spicy Zucchini Bread	111
Coconut Carrot Cookies	112
Rob's Pumpkin Muffins	113
Ultralight Peanut Butter Chocolate Chip Cookies	114
Mountain Muffins	115
World Cup Granola Bars	116
The Old Cookhouse Muffins	117
Whole Wheat Cakes with Cheese	118
Dog W.A.G. Biscuits	119

French Toast Ola La Monsieur !!

8 eggs
  salt & vanilla
200 ml. canned milk
12 slices french bread
 8 slices bacon
  almonds - toasted
  salted butter, icing sugar & maple syrup

Beat eggs in a bowl adding a touch of salt & vanilla. Add approx. 200 ml. milk & mix about 1 min. Dip each slice of bread into the egg & soak thoroughly. Stack slices & leave for about 10-15 min. Meanwhile, oven bake the bacon & toast the almonds.

Fry the prepared bread in butter over medium heat. Be careful not to brown the crust, for this makes it too firm. Turn.

Serve layered on a warm plate with butter, a generous sprinkling of icing sugar, topped off with the toasted almonds & 2 slices of bacon.

Serve warm maple syrup on the side.

Jim Gruetzke
Haus Heidi Pension

1

Dave Murray's Breakfast of Champions

3 c. water
1 c. slow cooking oatmeal
  pinch of sea salt
1 tbsp. sliced almonds
1 tbsp. pecans
2 tbsp. raisins
½ apple - diced
  sugar or maple syrup
  milk

Sometimes the simple things in life are the best!

Boil the water, salt added, in medium sized pot with lid.

Stir in oatmeal, nuts, raisins & apple. Simmer with lid on, stirring occasionally until thick.

Pour into bowls & add a small amount of brown sugar or maple syrup & milk.

Serves 2 hungry people. Porridge for breakfast may make you late for work, but it is worth it!

Dave Murray

Alpine Chalet Brunch

English muffins - toasted
fresh raw spinach - chopped fine
poached eggs
salt & freshly ground black pepper
butter
Parmesan
cayenne
lemon juice

Toast muffins while poaching eggs, keep hot in oven.

To assemble place muffin on a plate, top with spinach, poached egg, salt & pepper butter, Parmesan, cayenne & lemon juice in that order.

This recipe works well with scrambled eggs too.

Garnish with lemon wedges & serve with fresh fruit in season.

Alpine Chalet

Poppyseed Zucchini Impossible Pie

2 c. zucchini - chopped
1 large onion - finely diced
1 tbsp. butter
1 c. aged cheddar - grated
3 eggs
1½ c. milk
1 c. biscuit mix (or 1c. flour 2tsp. baking powder)
1 tsp. salt ½ tsp. ground pepper
1 tbsp. fines herbes
1 tbsp. poppy seed
1 clove garlic - minced

Sauté zucchini & onion in butter until tender. Remove from heat, add cheese. Put into a 10" pie plate (or leave in pan if it is a 10" pan.)

Blend remaining ingredients in blender for 30 seconds on high speed. Pour over zucchini & onion. Sprinkle with:
  1 tbsp. poppy seed & lots of parmesan
Bake 35+ min. at 400°. Let stand 10 min. before cutting. Serve with a green salad. Serves 6-8.

Diane Nicholson

4

Comfort Zone Waffles

1 c. flour
1 tsp. baking powder
½ tsp. baking soda
1 tbsp. oil
2 eggs - beaten
1 c. milk
yogurt, fresh fruit & maple syrup

Preheat waffle iron about 10 min. Combine the dry ingredients in a mixing bowl. Add oil, milk & eggs. Mix well.

Bake in waffle iron 10-12 min. until golden.

Serve hot, topped with yogurt, fresh fruit & maple syrup. 3-5 Servings.

Dave Feniak
The Comfort Zone Pension

5

California North Brunch

1 lb. Monterey Jack cheese - grated
1 lb. aged cheddar cheese - grated
1 8oz. tin green chilis, seeded & chopped
4 egg yolks - beaten
2/3 c. heavy cream
1 tbsp. flour
  salt & freshly ground black pepper
4 egg whites - stiffly beaten
2 tomatoes - sliced

Combine the cheeses & chilis & place in a buttered casserole (12" x 8" x 2").

In a small bowl combine egg yolks, cream, flour, salt & pepper & mix until well blended. Fold egg whites into the egg white mixture. Now pour over the cheese mixture in casserole.

Bake 30 min. at 350°. Remove & arrange tomato slices & return to oven for another 30 min.

Slice & serve with thick slices of sourdough toast & fresh fruit in season. Serves 6-8.

Priscilla Owen

6

Mogul Mountain Potatoes

1 2 lb. frozen hash browns
1 500 ml. sour cream
½ c. butter - melted
2 c. aged cheddar - grated
2 tins mushroom soup
1 large onion - chopped
  salt & freshly ground black pepper
1 tbsp. dill
  Parmesan

Mix all ingredients, except Parmesan, in a large bowl. Place in a large rectangular pan & top with lots of Parmesan & more grated cheddar. Bake at 350° for 1-1½ hrs.
  A great brunch dish & good with any meat, poultry or seafood. Serves 8

Maureen Provincal

7

Chalet Luise Swiss Muesli

1 c. raw oats
1 c. orange juice
  honey to taste & a few raisins
1 banana - sliced
2 pears - grated
  or any fruit in season
½ c. slivered almonds (or any nuts)
  cinnamon
  brown sugar
  yogurt & or whipped cream

  Soak oats, orange juice, honey & raisins at least 1 hr. or overnight.
  Put in bowls & top with bananas & pears. Sprinkle with almonds, cinnamon & brown sugar. Spoon over yogurt & or whipped cream.
  Great for breakfast, but also a healthy dessert.

                              Luise Zinsli
                              Chalet Luise

Our Famous Hawaiin Pizza

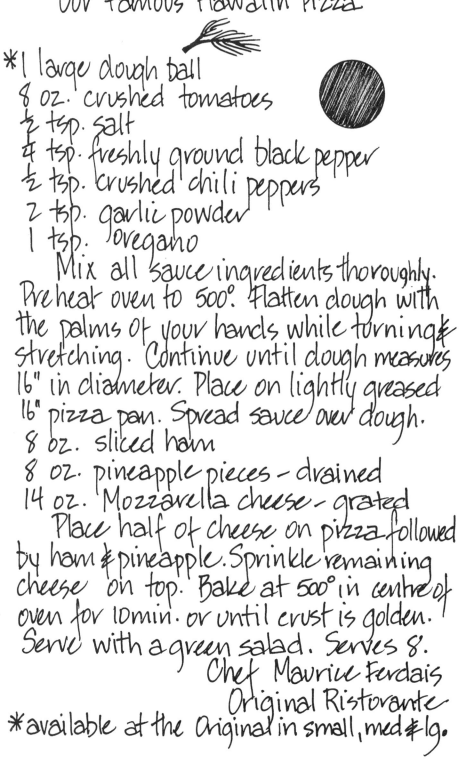

*1 large dough ball
  8 oz. crushed tomatoes
  ½ tsp. salt
  ¼ tsp. freshly ground black pepper
  ½ tsp. crushed chili peppers
  2 tsp. garlic powder
  1 tsp. oregano
  Mix all sauce ingredients thoroughly.
Preheat oven to 500°. Flatten dough with
the palms of your hands while turning &
stretching. Continue until dough measures
16" in diameter. Place on lightly greased
16" pizza pan. Spread sauce over dough.
  8 oz. sliced ham
  8 oz. pineapple pieces – drained
  14 oz. Mozzarella cheese – grated
  Place half of cheese on pizza followed
by ham & pineapple. Sprinkle remaining
cheese on top. Bake at 500° in centre of
oven for 10min. or until crust is golden.
Serve with a green salad. Serves 8.
                    Chef Maurice Ferdais
                    Original Ristorante
*available at the Original in small, med & lg.

9

Early Roman Paté

3 oz. tin tuna (or salmon)
2 tbsp. butter - melted
2 tsp. white wine
1 tbsp. vinegar
½ tsp. mustard seed / or coarse mustard
½ tsp. oregano
½ tsp. celery seed
1 tbsp. olive oil
1 tbsp. honey
pinch each basil, thyme & tarragon
1 mint leaf - chopped fine

Blend tuna & butter until smooth.
Add all ingredients & mix well. Spoon into
covered paté jar. Keep in fridge overnight.
Serve with French bread, assorted
cheeses at room temperature, grapes &
wine of course! Serves 2-4!

Diane Nicholson

10

Hot Crab & Dill Dip with Bread

½ lb. fresh crab
1 lg. pkg. cream cheese - softened
½ tsp. lemon juice
1 tsp. dill
1 tsp. horseradish
2-3 dashes Tabasco
slivered almonds
1 large round loaf rye bread

Cut top off the bread, hollow out, save pieces & cube for dipping.

Mix crab, cream cheese, lemon juice, dill, horseradish & Tabasco. Blend until smooth.

Spoon into hollow bread & top with almonds.

Bake at 350° for 40 min. Serve hot with the cubed bread for dipping.

Monica Weber

Parmesan Dill Taters

8 large potatoes - cubes
1 c. parmesan cheese
½ c. butter - melted
1 tsp. garlic salt
1 tsp. dill
1 tsp. lemon pepper
1 tsp. fresh parsley - chopped
1 tsp. fresh cilantro

Boil potatoes 5-8 min. until just tender.

Put potatoes, butter, cheese & all seasonings into a large flat casserole dish, mix well.

Bake at 500° until golden brown.

Great with Barry's Salsa Burgers or most casual meals... or by themselves!

Suzanne Minogue

My Favorite Stew

1½ lbs. beef chuck or round - 1" cubes
½ lb. bacon - cut into ½" pieces
1 large onion - sliced
3 tbsp. flour
4 c. hot beef consommé
1 large carrot - chopped
1 medium stalk celery - chopped
2 tomatoes - peeled & chopped
2 Bay leaves
salt & freshly ground pepper
1½ to 2 lbs potatoes, peeled - cut into pieces
½ c. chopped parsley
1 c. red wine

In a heavy skillet, sauté beef, bacon & onions over high heat until well browned. Transfer to a large pot. Stir flour into remaining fat in skillet. Cook, stirring constantly, until medium brown. Gradually add consommé, stirring until gravy is smooth. Pour over the meat & onions. Add vegetables & seasonings. Simmer, covered, abt. 1 hr. Add the potatoes & simmer until tender. For a little more zest, add wine during latter part of cooking. Garnish with parsley.

Peter Alder

Mountain Bike Greek Salad

1 bunch fresh oregano
250g. lambs Feta cheese
3 large ripe tomatoes
2 cucumbers
1 red pepper
1 yellow pepper
⅓ c. cold pressed virgin olive oil
olives ... your choice

Crumble Feta, cut tomatoes into wedges, chop cucumbers into bite-size pieces. Chop oregano finely & sprinkle over Feta, tomatoes, cucumbers. Slice the peppers thinly (with a cheese slicer) & add to salad. Now add olives of your choice. Pour the olive oil over salad but do not mix.

Put everything into a watertight container & into panniers. After a half day of riding, the salad will be well mixed!

Leanna Rath & Richard Kelly
Life Styles Adventure Company

14

Tapley's Famous Goulash

3 lbs. beef stew meat - cubed
1 lb. pork shoulder - cubed
   salt & freshly ground pepper to taste
1 large onion - diced
1 tbsp. vegetable oil
2-3 tbsp. flour
1 tbsp. each paprika, oregano & basil
3 Bay leaves
4 c. water
2 oz. dry red wine
1 beef boullion cube
2 tbsp. tomatoe paste
½ c. sour cream

Preheat electric pan to 350°. Add oil, salt
& pepper the meats. Brown meats & onions,
sprinkle with flour while stirring vigorously
Add seasonings. Brown flour, add water &
stir. Add wine, boullion & tomato paste. Cover
& reduce heat to 275°. Simmer 1½ hrs. stirring
occaisionally. Add water if necessary. Just
before serving blend in sour cream. Serve
over unpeeled & roasted garlic potatoes. Serves 8.

Tapley's Pub

Christopher's Srambled Tofu

1 454 g. pkg. tofu (sof) - crumbled
1 or 2 onions - diced
2 or 3 cloves garlic
   some mushrooms - fresh ones
2 stalks celery
   soya sauce - light
   cayenne

   Saute vegetables & tofu. Season
with soya sauce, cayenne & any green
stuff (herb) that tickles your fancy.
   Serve with a selection of fresh, steamed
vegetables & lemon wedges or... Not a
reccomended side dish with rare steaks
in other words. Serves 2-4
   Breakfast, lunch or dinner & good for ya!

                    Christopher Quirk

Nasty Jack's Chili Cheese Melts

½ lb. aged cheddar - grated
½ lb. mozzarella cheese - grated
1 small tin Ortega green chilies - chopped
2 cloves garlic - minced
2 c. real mayonnaise
   sourdough bread & black olives

Mix cheeses, chilies, garlic & mayonnaise in a small bowl.

Slice sourdough bread into thick slices, spread with the cheese mixture. Top with sliced black olives.

Bake at 325° until cheese melts.

This recipe makes lots, so freeze some on a cookie sheet, stack slices & store in plastic in the freezer. They don't need to be defrosted before baking.

Nasty Jack's

Leek & Pumpkin Soup

1 large leek - sliced thinly
4 tbsp. butter
1 tbsp. flour
2 c. pureed pumpkin
1 tsp. sugar
juice of 1 lemon
1½ c. chicken or vegetable stock
dash of tabasco
pinch of ground cloves
½ c. milk
salt & freshly ground black pepper

Saute leek with butter in a large pot. Sprinkle in flour. Add pumpkin, sugar, lemon juice, stock, & seasonings. Blend. Add milk. Blend. Heat slowly & simmer 5 min.

Pour into large, warmed soup bowls. Garnish with parmesan & a sprig of fresh parsley. Serve with any hearty bread. Serves 4.

Bev Ross

Barry's Salsa Burgers

2 lbs. lean ground beef
1 medium onion - diced
2 cloves garlic - chopped
   salt & freshly ground black pepper
8 large slices mozarella cheese
16 large slices summer sausage
4 tins sliced mushrooms
8 slices thick whole wheat bread
   real mayonnaise
   coarse ground mustard
   butter
   salsa sauce

In a small bowl, mix ground beef & onions. Form into 8 patties. Season with salt & pepper & insert small pieces of garlic into each. Fry & after flipping top with summer sausage & cheese. Remove when done & keep warm. Add mushrooms to pan & saute. Butter bread, add mayo, mustard, patties, salsa & mushrooms in that order. Serve open face, with beer. Serves 4-8.

Barry Johnston

19

Southside Hot Antipasto Hero

6" Baguettes
Vegetable antipasto - room temp.
Salami - sliced
Onion rings - thinly sliced
Tomatoes - sliced
Mozzarella cheese - sliced

Split baguettes lenthwise, toast tops until lightly browned. Spread thickly with antipasto, top with salami slices. Put a few onion slices on salami, then the tomatoes. Cover with cheese slices & sprinkle lightly with paprika & sweet basil.

Broil until cheese is bubbley & lightly browned. Best served with beer.

Olga
the Southside Deli

Cream of Ginger Carrot Soup

2 c. carrots - finely sliced
½ c. onions - chopped
1 c. water
3 chicken stock cubes
4 tbsp. butter
2 c. milk
1 tbsp. lemon juice
2 tbsp. ea. flour & sugar
¼ tsp. ginger

Simmer carrots, onions, water, chicken stock cubes & butter until carrots are tender. Cool slightly. Pureé in blender, add remaining ingredients & blend. Return to pot & simmer until thickened, stirring occasionally. Add additional milk for the consistancy you like. Season with salt & freshly ground pepper to taste.

Serve in warmed soup bowls, garnish with lemon wedges, fresh parsley & a bit of sour cream or yogurt.

Carlyne Brunner

The Hot Gourmet

assorted cold cuts (good sausage & ham etc.)
real mayonnaise
cream cheese - softened
green onion - chopped
freshly ground black pepper
fresh sourdough or rye bread
hot mustard, Edam cheese & dill pickles

Slice cold cuts very thinly (⅛") Put in a small bowl, add enough mayonnaise to coat cold cuts. Add a little cream cheese, green onion & pepper. Mix.
Slice bread into thick slices, spread with hot mustard. Spoon meat mixture over & top with a slice of Edam & a long slice of dill pickle.
Bake in oven, microwave or toaster oven till cheese melts.
Make lots & freeze them on a cookie sheet, stack in freezer bags & bake unthawed. Great, fast après ski - apre anything!

The Gourmet

Shrimp Gazpacho Araxi

2 onions
1 green pepper
2 carrots
3-4 cloves garlic-minced
6 tomato-concasses
1 tin Clamato juice
2 tbsp. basil
2 tbsp. oregano
  Lea & Perrins
  salt & fresh, coarse black pepper
1 tbsp. sugar
  small shrimp
  lemon slices & chopped parsley

Mince vegetables in food processer (do not purée) Add to tomatoes & Clamato juice. Add all seasonings to taste. Let sit 6-8 hrs.

To serve fill a tall dessert glass with the gazpacho. Top with 6-7 small shrimp, a twist of lemon & chopped parsley. Serves 6-8.

Chef Warren Grommada
Araxi's

23

Smoked Oysters in Soy Sauce

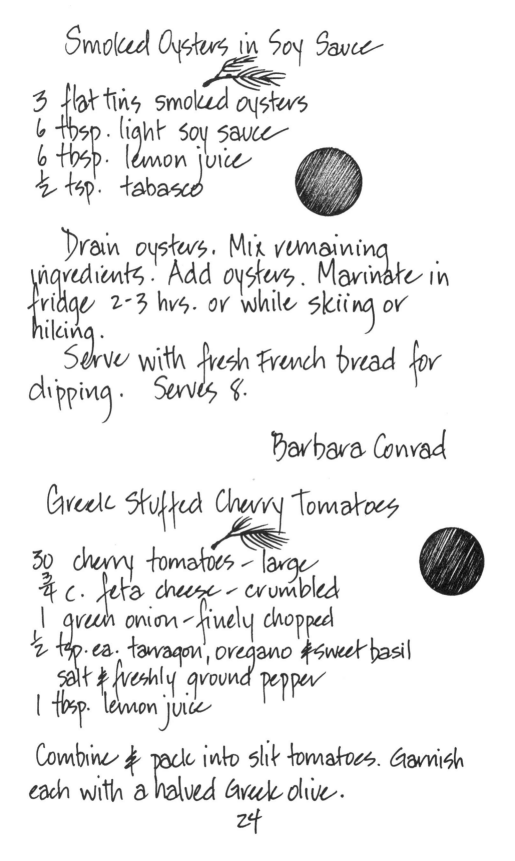

3 flat tins smoked oysters
6 tbsp. light soy sauce
6 tbsp. lemon juice
½ tsp. tabasco

Drain oysters. Mix remaining ingredients. Add oysters. Marinate in fridge 2-3 hrs. or while skiing or hiking.
Serve with fresh French bread for dipping. Serves 8.

Barbara Conrad

Greek Stuffed Cherry Tomatoes

30 cherry tomatoes - large
¾ c. feta cheese - crumbled
1 green onion - finely chopped
½ tsp. ea. tarragon, oregano & sweet basil
salt & freshly ground pepper
1 tbsp. lemon juice

Combine & pack into slit tomatoes. Garnish each with a halved Greek olive.

Cantina Wings Con Pina

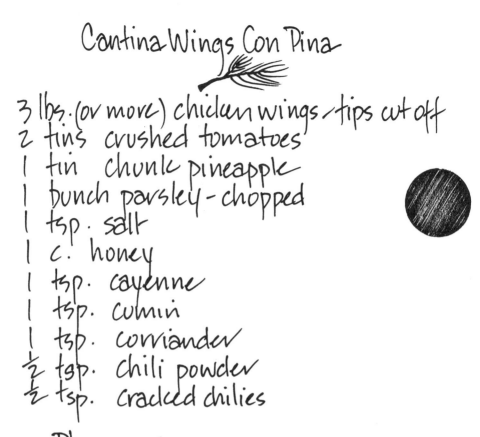

3 lbs. (or more) chicken wings, tips cut off
2 tins crushed tomatoes
1 tin chunk pineapple
1 bunch parsley - chopped
1 tsp. salt
1 c. honey
1 tsp. cayenne
1 tsp. cumin
1 tsp. corriander
½ tsp. chili powder
½ tsp. cracked chilies

Place wings in a large rectangular pan. Mix all ingredients in a large bowl & pour over wings. Bake at 450° for about 45 min.

Serve with warm tortillas & a green salad... & cervasa of course! Serves 4 as a main course & serves 10 as an appetizer.

Chef Teck McLaren
Dusty's Cantina

Araxi's Creamy Vinaigrette & Greens

¼ c. sour cream
¼ c. mayonnaise
2-3 cloves garlic - crushed
   salt & freshly ground black pepper
   Tabasco
¼ c. olive oil.

Blend all ingredients except olive oil in a large bowl with a flexible whisk. Slowly, a bit at a time, blend in the olive oil.

butter lettuce - torn
Romaine - torn
spinach - torn
mushrooms - sliced

Arrange on individual salad plates & spoon the vinaigrette over.
Garnish with sliced hard boiled eggs & sliced red peppers.

Chef Warren Grommada
Araxis

Indonesian Peanut Sauce with Vegetables

3 tsp. oil
1 350 g. jar peanut butter
½ tsp. freshly ground black pepper
½ tsp. ginger powder
½ tsp. curry powder
1 litre cold water
¼ c. soya sauce
3 tbsp. brown sugar
a selection of fresh vegetables - sliced cauliflower, broccoli, carrots, mushrooms, zucchini, snow peas, green & red peppers.

Heat oil, add peanut butter & spices, stir 3 min. Add water & stir until sauce is smooth. Add soya sauce & brown sugar. Bring slowly to the boil.

Arrange vegetables on a large platter. Serve with warm or cold peanut sauce in individual bowls.

This sauce is also excellent with chicken, beef or pork kebabs as a main course, served with rice.

Ted Nebbeling

Honey & Garlic Prawns

½ c. butter
½ c. honey
2 lbs. prawns - shelled
½ clove garlic - crushed
  lemon wedges

Melt butter in sauce pan, add honey & garlic. Add prawns & sauté 3 min. Do not overcook!

Garnish with lemon wedges & serve over a bed of hot, fluffy rice. Accompany with fresh vegetables in season. Serves 4.

Very good & very easy!

The Whistler Seafood Corp.

Made in Greece Satziki

1 500g. pkg. plain yogurt
1 250g. pkg. cream cheese
½ cucumber
1-2 cloves garlic - crushed
1 green onion, fresh chives & or mint
lemon juice
salt & freshly ground black pepper
pita bread, lemon wedges

At least 4 hrs. before serving, empty yogurt into a square of muslin (or a new J-cloth will do fine) & tie into a bundle. Suspend over a bowl & drain 4 hrs. or overnight. A very important step for texture... & authenticity
Grate cucumber onto a large plate & sprinkle with salt (liberally). Tilt plate to allow the juice to drain.
Beat the cream cheese & yogurt together, add garlic, green onion, chives & or mint. Add lemon juice, salt & pepper to taste.
Serve with warm pita bread & lemon wedges. Serves 6-8. A must with any Greek dish.

Janine Gavin

29

Priscilla's Artichoke Dip

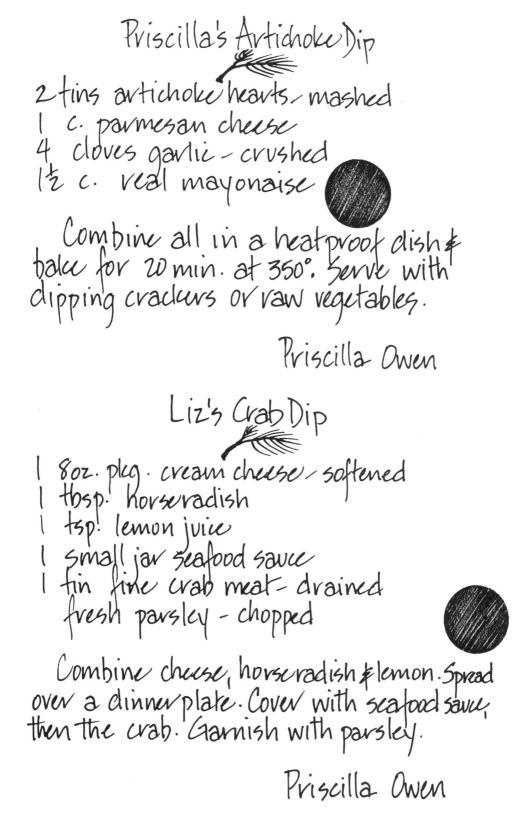

2 tins artichoke hearts - mashed
1 c. parmesan cheese
4 cloves garlic - crushed
1½ c. real mayonaise

Combine all in a heatproof dish &
bake for 20 min. at 350°. Serve with
dipping crackers or raw vegetables.

Priscilla Owen

Liz's Crab Dip

1 8oz. pkg. cream cheese - softened
1 tbsp. horseradish
1 tsp. lemon juice
1 small jar seafood sauce
1 tin fine crab meat - drained
fresh parsley - chopped

Combine cheese, horseradish & lemon. Spread
over a dinner plate. Cover with seafood sauce,
then the crab. Garnish with parsley.

Priscilla Owen

Artichoke Amour

21 saltine crackers - crushed
1 bunch green onions - chopped
4 eggs - beaten
2 small jars artichoke hearts - chopped
1½ c. aged cheddar - grated
1 c. fresh mushrooms - sliced
¼ tsp. cayenne pepper

Lightly grease 8"x8" glass pan. Mix all ingredients together & pour into pan. Bake at 350° for 35-40 min.
Cool. Cut into 1½" squares & place on a platter decorated with Romaine lettuce & black olives. Serves 12.

Elin (Sam) Sigmundson

Great hot too! Serves 4 as a main course for breakfast, lunch, or dinner.

Note: marinated artichoke hearts are best.

Acapulco North Ceviche

1 litre lime juice
3 whole cloves
1½ tbsp. garlic puree
4 red peppers - julienne
8 each Jalapeño & sweet green chilies - julienne
1½ bunchs cilantro
4 tomato concasse
salt & freshly ground black pepper
Combine in a large bowl. Set aside.

1 lb. scallops
1 lb. salmon
1 lb. sole
1 lb. prawns
1 lb. shrimp
1 c. olive oil
Slice seafood into 1" x 4" slices except shrimp.
Pour marinade over seafood & let sit 15 min.
Cover with olive oil & let marinate 4 hours.
to serve scoop into 6 oz. glasses.
Garnish with a sprig of cilantro & a
lime wedge. Serves many!

Chef Dan Atkinson
Planters at the International Lodge

32

Asparagus Mousse

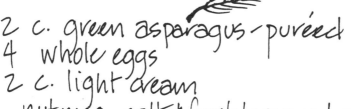

2 c. green asparagus - puréed
4 whole eggs
2 c. light cream
   nutmeg, salt & freshly ground pepper

Beat eggs in a stainless steel bowl. Add 1 c. light cream & pour into asparagus purée, season to taste with nutmeg, salt & pepper.

Pour into 4-6 buttered timbales & place in hot bain-marie. Bake at 275° to 300° for 20-25 min. Remove & cool for 2-4 hrs.

To remove mousse, insert a knife around edge of the timbale & invert onto serving plate.

Garnish with chiffonade of lettuce & julienne of carrot & topped with julienne of blanched orange rind. Serves 4-6.

Ideal first course for Chicken with Watercress & Ginger Sauce. P. 41

Chef Mickel Clayton
Chez Joël

Pika Seafood in Puff Pastry

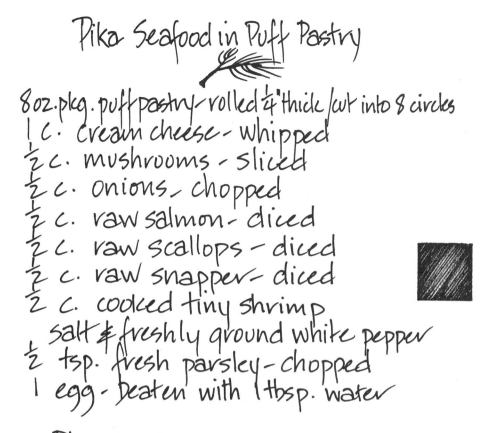

8 oz. pkg. puff pastry - rolled ¼" thick /cut into 8 circles
1 c. cream cheese - whipped
½ c. mushrooms - sliced
½ c. onions - chopped
½ c. raw salmon - diced
½ c. raw scallops - diced
½ c. raw snapper - diced
2 c. cooked tiny shrimp
  salt & freshly ground white pepper
½ tsp. fresh parsley - chopped
1 egg - beaten with 1 tbsp. water

Place 4 puff pastry rounds on a greased baking sheet. Combine all ingredients, except egg, in a bowl. Put ¼ of this mixture in the middle of each round. Brush egg wash around the outer edge of pastry. Place the other rounds on top. Crimp together.

Bake at 375° for about 30-45 min or until pastry is done.

Serves 2 as a main course or 4 as an appetizer.

Chef Michel Bertholet
Pika's

Roast Carrot & Brie Soup

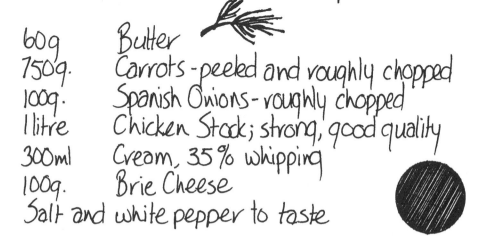

60g	Butter
750g.	Carrots - peeled and roughly chopped
100g.	Spanish Onions - roughly chopped
1 litre	Chicken Stock; strong, good quality
300ml	Cream, 35% whipping
100g.	Brie Cheese

Salt and white pepper to taste

Roast carrots in butter in oven until brown. Tranfer to saute pan and sweat with onions, until onions are translucent (clear). Season to taste with salt and pepper. Add chicken stock. Simmer for 45 min. to 1 hour, until soft. Place in work bowl of food processor and blend in small amounts of Brie cheese at a time. Adjust thickness with chicken stock. Add desired cream and seasoning of salt and pepper. Suggested rolls or breads:
- Salted herb-crusted baguettes or light cornbread biscuit.

Bernard C. Casavant
Executive Chef

Rodney Butters
Executive Sous Chef

Chateau Whistler Resort

Shitake and Scallops

-Total cooking time 6 min - Serves 4

12 oz.	shitake mushroom (slice shitake)
12 oz.	scallops
2 tsp.	butter
1 tsp.	lemon juice
1/4 tsp.	salt
1/8 tsp.	white pepper
1 tblsp.	sake
2 tsp.	soya sauce

First time spreading oil on the Teppan grill, set the heat on medium high. Wait for smoke to come out, then place shitake and scallops on the Teppan grill.
Season a little bit of salt & pepper on the shitake and scallops. Cook scallops two min. until a nice colour. Now place shitake and scallop together. Add seasoning & melted butter, add soya sauce, sake, lemon juice and serve.

Chef - Le at Teppan Village

Mulligatawny Soup-Sweet Chicken Curry Soup

-Feeds 10-12 people as a starter

1 boneless chicken breast, skin removed, diced
1½-2 litres water
1 medium onion diced
2 medium carrots diced
2 stalks celery diced
1 large potato diced
1 red pepper diced
1 green pepper diced
1 apple diced
1 banana diced
1 lime cut in half
1 7oz can pineapple pieces
  strawberries to garnish
Sm. bunch cilantro-chopped, 1 bay leaf, 1 tsp.
whole thyme, 2-3 tblsp. curry powder or to
taste, 1 tsp. cumin, pinch of tumeric for colour
*1 tsp. sambal
salt & pepper to taste   *special items
1 tblsp. finely dried ginger   available at
* 400ml can of coconut milk   Hatto's

cont'd

250 gr. low fat yogurt
250 gr. buttermilk
2 tblsp. butter
2 cups cooked rice

Sauté onions in butter, add curry powder, let simmer for 2 min., add chicken, sambal, cumin, tumeric, salt, pepper, ginger, bay leaf, thyme, lime halves and water. Let come to a boil then bring down to a simmer for 20-30 min. on low heat. Add carrots, celery, & potatoes. When potatoes are done add peppers, apple, banana, pineapple pieces and juice, add chopped cilantro. Combine coconut milk, yogurt, buttermilk, mix well. Stir mixture into soup, let come to a boil. Scoop all excess foam from top of soup. Turn off to prevent Dairy products from curdling. To serve add cooked rice and garnish with a little yogurt, cilantro & strawberries. If you like it hot add crushed chillies or Sambal.

Enjoy!
Hatto's
Corner Deli

the team,
Roberta, Hatto,
Brenda

Moules Marinière

4 lbs. mussels
2 bunches parsley - chopped
6 oz. shallots - chopped
3 oz. garlic - chopped fine
½ litre dry white wine
2 tbsp. butter
½ litre whipping cream
  salt, pepper, bay leaf & Tabasco

Clean all mussels individually. Melt butter in a large pot, add ½ parsley, shallots, & garlic. Add wine, bring to a boil over high heat. Add salt, pepper, bay leaf plus a touch of Tabasco. Add all mussels, cover & cook 5 min. on high heat.

Drain liquid into a shallow pan, set mussels aside & keep warm. Add whipping cream & balance of parsley to the liquid. Cook approx. 10 min. until sauce thickens.

Add mussels back in the pot. Cook 2 min. at medium heat. Et voila!

Bon Appetit — Pascal
— Herb / Les Deux
Gros Ristaurante

39

Jean Pierre's Sole Pecheur

Shrimp - diced
Scallops - diced # filets of sole
Shallots - chopped
Mushrooms - diced
Brandy
Heavy cream
White wine & fish stock or water
Salt & pepper, herbs
Egg yolk

Lightly sauté seafood, shallots & mushrooms in butter. Season to taste & deglaze pan with brandy. Make a paste of these ingredients using a little cream to bind.

Sandwich the paste between 2 sole filets & poach gently in a shallow covered pan, in wine & water (fish stock is preferrable to the water)

Remove & keep warm. Reduce liquid by half, add cream & reduce by half again. Season to taste. Remove pan from heat & whisk in an egg yolk & just before serving incorporate a heaping tablespoon of whipped cream.

Chef Jean Pierre Dandurand/Blackcomb Mt.

40

Louisiana North Barbecued Shrimp

1 tsp. each cayenne & black pepper
½ tsp. each crushed red peppers, thyme & oregano
¼ tsp. salt
Combine this seasoning mix in a small bowl.

14 large fresh shrimp - headless
¼ lb. plus 5 tbsp. butter - room temperature
1½ tsp. garlic - minced
2 tbsp. fresh rosemary - chopped
1 tbsp. black pepper
1 tsp. Worcestershire
½ c. shrimp or fish stock
¼ c. beer - room temperature

Split shrimp & remove back vein. In a large skillet, over high heat, combine 5 tbsp. butter, seasoning mix & other seasonings. Add shrimp & saute 2 min. (shake pan in back & forth motion) Add stock, simmer 2 min. Add beer & shake 1 min. Add remaining butter, shaking pan until all butter is amalgamated.

Garnish with parsley & serve with rice & a green salad. Serves 2.

Chef Frank Ziewitz

Jansson's Frestelse/Swedish Potatoes

2-3 onions - thinly sliced
   butter
4-5 large potatoes - peeled & sliced ¼" thick
2 tins Swedish or Norwegin anchovies
1½ c. cream

The trick to this dish is to use Swedish or Norwegian anchovies. If temporarily unavailable locally they can be found in IKEA's food dept.
   Pre heat oven to 375°. Quarter potato slices.
   Saute the onions until golden, not brown. Layer the potatoes, onions & anchovies in a buttered dish, starting & ending with the potatoes. Dot with butter.
   Bake 10 min. Pour half of the cream over & return to oven for 10 min. Add remaining cream & bake about 40 min. until potatoes are tender. Serve with pickles, fresh vegetables in season & green salad. Serves 4.
   I first enjoyed this dish in Lappland during a ski trip in the midnight sun.

Stephanie Sloan

Ty's Saskatchewan Lobster

6 whole 4 lb. live Atlantic lobster
6 bottles expensive white wine
4 lb. or so butter melted
fresh lemon & garlic — the usual.

Heat 1 bottle of wine in a large pot while considering the problem of dealing with certain death for those poor lobsters.

You may want to have a few glasses of wine for this part. You will then probably come to the conclusion that the wine (in the pot) will probably make things a little easier for the lobsters too.

Plunge lobsters into the pot — <u>don't look!</u> Sit down & drink a few more glasses of wine quickly 3-5 min. max. Remove lobsters from wine — note that actually they don't look too bad at all. Serve with the butter flavoured with garlic & lemon. Serves 6.

Share the rest of the wine with your friends that have shared your experience. Resolve to buy frozen ones next time.

Ty Watts

43

Lu Garden Black Pepper Steak

1 lb. beef tenderloin, sliced diagonally ¼" thick
1 tsp. soda & 1 tbsp. water
   Mix & set aside 2 hrs. Wash & wipe dry.

½ tsp. sugar
2 tsp. potato starch
2 tbsp. each wine, light soya sauce & water
2 tsp. each shallot & garlic, chopped
   Combine & marinate beef for ½ hr., then
Stir fry over low heat until medium rare.
Set aside.

1 tbsp. each oil, oyster sauce & dark soya sauce
2 tsp. coarsly ground black pepper
1 tsp. each sugar & tomato sauce
3 tbsp. water
   Combine in wok over high heat, add beef
& stir fry until just cooked. Place on platter.

1 small onion & 1 each red & green pepper, sliced
   Stir fry briefly. Place over beef & serve
with rice & steamed vegetables. Serves 2-4.

Chef Ghoi Wong
Lu Garden

44

Chicken Breasts with Watercress & Ginger

1 bunch watercress - chopped
¼ lb. butter
8 chicken breasts - skinned
  flour
  salt & freshly ground pepper
2 tbsp. butter
2 tbsp. fresh ginger - julienne
2 c. heavy cream.

Purée the watercress with the butter.
Place in a small bowl & keep cool.
    Season chicken breasts with salt &
pepper. Dust with flour & sauté over medium
heat until light brown on both sides.
Finish in the oven at 400° for 8-10 min.
    Sauté ginger in butter 2-3 min. over
low heat, add cream & reduce by half.
When ready to serve, bring sauce to a
boil, & add the watercress butter a little at
a time. Check seasoning & serve with
fresh vegetables in season & a green salad.
Serves 4.

Chef Mikel Clayton
Chez Joël

45

Don's Squash & Cheddar Casserole

3 c. squash – cubed & cooked
6 c. cooked rice
½ c. onion – finely chopped
¼ c. sunflower seeds
¼ c. sesame seeds
garlic, thyme & oregano – to taste

Combine above ingredients in a casserole dish.

2 c. yogurt
¼ c. sunflower seed oil
½ c. aged Cheddar
1 egg – beaten

Heat slowly, yogurt, oil & cheese. Remove from heat & add egg. Blend. Pour sauce over casserole, sprinkle with more garlic, thyme, oregano & a little butter. Cook for 40 min. at 350°. Serve with a large green salad. Serves 6.

Don Barr

46

Escalopes of Salmon

1 litre	heavy cream
10	eggs yolks
4 oz.	Vermouth
1 cup	whole fresh basil leaves
1 side	fresh salmon.

Bring cream to boil and let cool. Mix yolks, vermouth and basil leaves. Add cooled cream to glaze. Place glaze on plate and arrange salmon slice in desired pattern. Broil until salmon is cooked - about 45 sec. Garnish with small basil leaf.

Bruce Knapik
Executive Chef
Twig's Restaurant
Delta Mountain Inn

Beef Bourguignon René

4 lbs. beef - cubed
¼ lb. bacon - sliced
2 tbsp. oil
1 large carrot - sliced
1 bunch shallots - chopped
1 large onion - cubed
5 tbsp. flour
   salt & freshly ground black pepper
1 clove garlic - crushed
1 litre red wine
1 bunch parsley - chopped
3 Bay leaves & thyme to taste

Saute the beef & bacon, in another skillet
saute the carrots, shallots & onion in oil.
Combine with the meat. Dust with flour, season
with salt & pepper & bake at 350° for 5-10 min.
until the flour colours a bit. Add the garlic, wet
with the red wine, add the parsley & herbs &
simmer 30 min. Add a little water & bake 1½ hr.
at 350°. Serve over fettucini & with fresh
vegetables in season or a green salad. Serves 6

Chef René Brachet
Chez Joël

48

Fettuccine with Asparagus

1 lb. fettucine
2 lbs. fresh asparagus
1/4 c. butter
1 c. whipping cream
salt & freshly ground black pepper
1/4 c. Parmesan cheese - grated
2 tbsp. fresh parsley - finely chopped

Cook fettucine al dente 3-5 min. for fresh, 5-7 min. for dry fettucine.
Tie asparagus & blanch in boiling salted water 2 min. Drain, rinse in cold water & set aside. When cool, cut off tips.
Gently sauté asparagus in butter over medium heat 1-2 min. Add cream, heat till cream begins to bubble. Season with salt & pepper.
Add fettuccine, toss gently & heat. Gradually add Parmesan, toss & heat till cheese has melted.
Sprinkle with parsley & serve. Serves 4-6.

The Managment & Staff
Trattoria di Umberto

Coriander, Cornmeal Crusted Boston Blue; Ragout of Beans & Grains

For the beans: (All are pre-cooked seperately);
Yield: 4 servings

250g.	Red Onions, diced
100 g.	Pinto Beans
100g.	Black Eyed Peas
50g.	Yellow Lentils
50g.	Red Lentils
20g.	Roasted Garlic, crushed, minced
50ml.	Grain Mustard

For the Vinaigrette:

60 mls.	Tarragon Vinegar
180 mls.	Olive Oil
30gms.	Shallots, minced
To taste	Salt and milled pepper

For each Plate:
Hearts of Curly Endive or Flowering Kale
Diced Tomatoes (Concasse)
Coriander Leaves

Cont.

cont.

For the Boston Blue:

20g.	Minced Coriander (Reserve 4-5 leaves for plate garnish)
10g.	Finely Minced Jalepeno Peppers
250g.	Cornmeal
150-180g.	Boston Blue (per serving)
120ml.	Mixture of Butter, Vegetable Oil (for frying)

Suggestion Presentation:

Prepare the ragout by first sauteing the red onions, then adding in the beans, grains, garlic, mustard and peppers. Next, add in the vinaigrette; remove from heat and keep warm. Pan fry the fish; then place the greens in the centre of the plate, placing the ragout around the perimeter, then the fried fish on top of the greens. Sprinkle the diced tomato, coriander leaves and serve at once.

Cheers,

Bernard C. Casavant   Trevor Jackson
Executive Chef   Banquet Chef
        Chateau Whistler Resort

Fettucini with Clam & Basil Sauce

1 tin baby clams
1 small onion - finely chopped
1-2 cloves garlic - finely chopped
2 tbsp. fresh basil - finely chopped
¾ c. light cream
fresh parsley
freshly ground black pepper
Parmesan cheese

Drain clams, reserving the liquor. In a little butter saute' the onions & garlic until limp. Add clam liquor & simmer until reduced by half. Add cream & basil & simmer until sauce is slightly thickened. Add clams & heat. Prepare fettucini for 2 - al dente.

Pour clam & basil sauce over fettucini, garnish with parsley, pepper & Parmesan.

Serve with a spinich salad & lemon wedges. Serves 2.

Darla Gauthier

Michael's Gone Fishin' Ginger Salmon

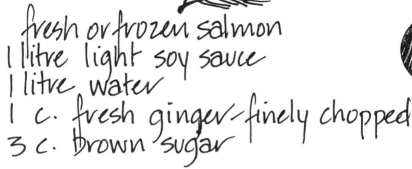

fresh or frozen salmon
1 litre light soy sauce
1 litre water
1 c. fresh ginger — finely chopped
3 c. brown sugar

Mix soy, water, ginger & sugar together. Let stand 6 hrs. or overnight. Cut salmon into 1" steaks. Marinate in soy & ginger marinade for about 6 hours ... or while skiing, hiking or fishing.

Remove, barbecue or broil 7 min. first side & 5 min. second side. Do not overcook, salmon should be moist & flakey — not dry.

Garnish with fresh ginger, lemon slices & parsley.

Serve with rice & fresh vegetables in season.

Michael Davies
Green River Fishing Guides

Mountain Stream Trout with Orange & Tarragon

4 whole fresh trout
salt & pepper (to taste)
juice of 1 lemon
4 slices of orange
4 large sprigs fresh tarragon
flour (to dust)
6 tbsp. olive oil
3 tbsp. butter
juice of 1 orange

Preheat oven to 350°. Rinse trout under cold running water & pat dry.
Season with salt & pepper. Sprinkle with lemon juice. Stuff each trout with 1 orange slice & lay 1 sprig of tarragon over each slice. Dust with flour.
Saute trout in oil & butter 2-3 min. per side, remove & place on buttered baking dish. Sprinkle with orange juice. Bake 8 min.
Remove from oven & place trout on a platter. Set aside & keep warm.

cont.

Orange & Tarragon Sauce

4 tbsp. butter
juice of 1 orange
juice of ½ lemon
5 tbsp. dry white wine
1 tbsp. fresh tarragon - finely chopped
1 tsp. fresh parsley - finely chopped
8 orange slices, peeled & seeded.

Melt butter in a skillet. Add orange juice & white wine & blend in. Add tarragon & parsley & stir in. Add orange slices & heat to warm.

Spoon sauce over trout on platter - 2 orange slices per trout & serve immediately from platter to individual plates. Serves 4.

The Managment & Staff
Il Caminetto Di Umberto

Isabelle's Beef Dijon

12 oz. beef tenderlion – cut in 6 slices
3 oz. butter – clarified
6 tbsp. Dijon Reine mustard
4 c. whipping cream

Melt clarified butter in a saucepan over high heat. Saute beef until brown on both sides. Set aside.

Using a wire whisk distribute the Dijon mustard well in the saucepan. Pour in the whipping cream & whisk thoroughy. Reduce heat & cook until the sauce is thick & creamy.

Add beef & let cook for a few minutes, should be rare to medium rare.

Place beef on a warmed platter & pour the sauce over.

Serve with potatoes & an assortment of fresh steamed vegetables.

Chef Monika Czerveniak
Isabelle's

Ambrosia's Chicken Oscar

6 oz.	chicken breast
3 oz.	dungeness crabmeat
4	asparagus spears
2	egg yolks
4 oz	white wine
8 oz.	clarified butter
½	lemon
	salt & pepper

Remove all fat and skin from chicken and poach in 2 oz. white wine. Add 2 oz water for aprox. 8 min in 450° oven. Remove from liquid and place on a pie plate. Sauté asparagus and place on chicken breast. Then put on the crabmeat leaving the tips showing. Top with Hollandaise sauce. Bake 5 min. in 450° oven.

cont'd.

cont'd

Hollandaise Sauce:

Put egg yolks and remaining white wine into a stainless steel bowl. Place over a pot of boiling water and beat vigorously with a whisk until mixture becomes frothy (remove from heat immediately, don't overcook). Pour in clarified butter in a stream 8 inches above, while stirring constantly (Pour slowly for best results). Squeeze in lemon, salt and pepper to taste.

Voila!

P.S. Add crushed garlic, port wine and parmesan cheese to leftover Hollandaise sauce for a beautiful accompaniment to sautéed zucchini or broccoli.

The Chefs at Ambrosia
in Nancy Green Lodge

Pheasant with Mountain Blueberries

2 pheasant breasts - deboned
salt & flour
clarified butter
2 oz. Blueberry wine or medium sherry
3 oz. demie glaze
fresh or frozen blueberries

Preheat oven to 350°. Roll pheasant breasts in flour & salt. Saute in butter till browned. Bake at 350° for 15 min. (Be careful, pheasant dries quickly)
. Remove from pan & deglaze pan with wine or sherry. Add demie glaze & blueberries. Heat.
Place breasts on warmed plates & spoon sauce over. Serve with wild rice & fresh vegetables in season.

Chef Fernand Desroches
Myrtles at the Timberline Lodge

Tempura Toshi

Tempura Batter: 2 c. water - very cold
2 egg yolks
2 c. pastry flour - sift 2-3 times

Lightly beat together water & egg yolks. Add flour gradually, beat lightly. Batter should not be over beaten, delicately & lightly is the secret of sucess. Place batter in a bowl of ice.

A selection of: shrimps, scallops, cod & salmon - all bite size! Carrot, squash, sweet potato, snow peas, green pepper, egg plant & zuchini, or... all sliced & dry.

Pour vegetable oil 3" deep in a deep 10-12" skillet. Heat oil to 350°. (use thermometer)

Dust all seafood & vegetables with flour & dip in batter! Place in oil one at a time, until only ⅔ of oil surface is covered, to keep temperature high. Drop a little more batter on each piece. This will make them crispier & beautiful. Fry 2-3 min. each side. Remove & shake well.

cont.

Tempura Sauce: ½ c. soy sauce
½ c. rice wine or saki
2 c. Japanese fish stock
sugar to taste

Mix in a small saucepan. Bring to a boil & remove from heat.
Garnish with grated white radish & sliced ginger root.

Arrange tempura attractivly on individual wood or pottery platters with a small bowl of Tempura sauce on the side.

Serve with rice & warmed saki. (Remember to never serve your own saki - its bad manners!)

Chef Toshi Saito
Sushi Villiage

From Our Hot Rock Cafe; La Fiesta

Marinated Artichokes, Prosciutto Ham, Balsamic Vinegar

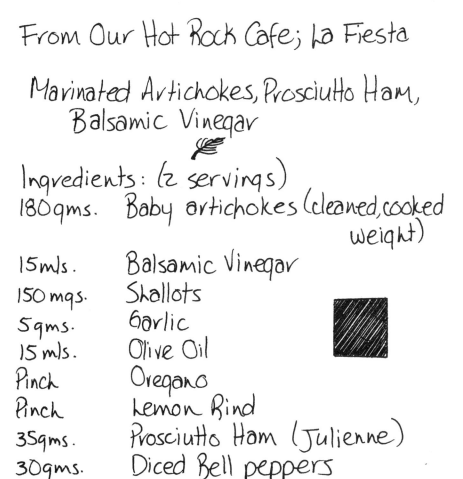

Ingredients: (2 servings)

180 gms.   Baby artichokes (cleaned, cooked weight)

15 mls.	Balsamic Vinegar
150 mgs.	Shallots
5 gms.	Garlic
15 mls.	Olive Oil
Pinch	Oregano
Pinch	Lemon Rind
35 gms.	Prosciutto Ham (Julienne)
30 gms.	Diced Bell peppers
to taste	Salt and Pepper

The day previous, clean and cook the artichokes as per a classical recipe book. Cut the artichokes, the prosciutto ham, the peppers and combine in a bowl.

cont.

cont.

Prepare the vinaigrette, adding all of the remaining items and whisking thoroughly. Pour over artichoke mixture, let stand in refrigerator for 2-3 hours, covered tightly. Toss just before serving; either on individual plates or on a platter over some brightly coloured lettuce or perhaps with toasted pita bread.

Ideally functional for an easy, casual good time; "Tapas" style.

Enjoy!

Bernard C. Casavant   Stephen French
Executive Chef   Restaurant Chef
    Chateau Whistler Resort

Black Forest Chicken Hunter Style

2 half chickens (breast & leg) de boned
¼ c. bacon - diced
   oil
1 small onion - finely diced
10 medium mushrooms - sliced
6 small pearl onions
1 clove garlic - finely chopped
   salt, pepper & paprika to taste
1 oz. red wine
1 c. chicken stock

Dust chicken with flour. Sauté in oil with bacon, until golden brown. Remove from pan & set aside. Sauté onion, mushrooms, pearl onions & garlic. Add seasonings to taste. Add red wine & chicken stock. Return chicken to pan & bake at 375° for 25 min.

Serve with spätzel (homemade noodles) or any flat egg noodles & vegetable of your choice. Serves 2.

Chef Herb Neiman
Black Forest

64

Montreal West Tortiéve

1 good pie crust (top & bottom)
2 lbs. ground pork
2 small onions - chopped
½ c. boiling water
1 clove garlic - minced
  salt & freshly ground black pepper
1 tsp. sage
¼ tsp. celery salt
⅛ tsp. ground cloves
  sherry
3 medium potatoes - mashed

Prepare crust & place in pie plate. Saute all ingredients, except the potatoes, over medium heat for about 45 min. Be sure it doesn't get too dry - add more sherry!
Mix in the mashed potatoes & place in the pie crust & top with second crust.
Bake at 450° for 10 min. & then lower temperature to 375° & finish baking for 35-40 min.
Serve with homemade pickles.

Priscilla Owen

Wild Flower Vinegar

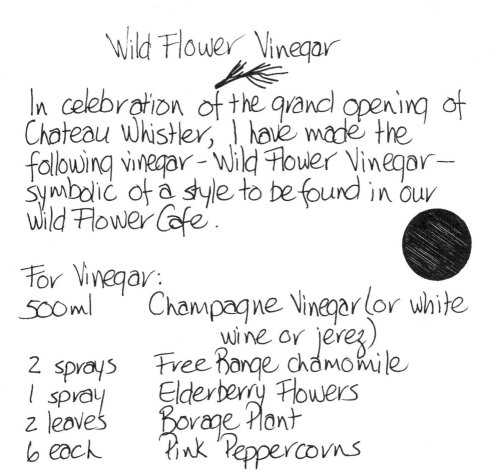

In celebration of the grand opening of Chateau Whistler, I have made the following vinegar – Wild Flower Vinegar – symbolic of a style to be found in our Wild Flower Cafe.

For Vinegar:

500ml	Champagne Vinegar (or white wine or jerez)
2 sprays	Free Range chamomile
1 spray	Elderberry Flowers
2 leaves	Borage Plant
6 each	Pink Peppercorns

Put all herbs into bottle, bring vinegar to boil, pour into bottle. Allow to cool, cork and seal with paraffin wax. Must be allowed to mature 2-3 weeks. When using the vinegar, it must be strained.

cont.

For the Vinaigrette - 2 Servings

15gms.	French Purple Shallots, minced
60 mls.	Wild Flower Vinegar
180 mls.	Grapeseed Oil
To taste	Salt & Pepper
1 tsp.	Flowing Thyme, minced

Combine all ingredients, whisking together to form a thick dressing.

Suggested Servings for Salads:

* Fresh grated zucchini with shrimp meat, radicchio leaves.
* Roma tomatoes, bococcinni cheese, Wild Flower Vinaigrette
* Carpaccio of scallops; salad roll of greens, Wild Flower Vinaigrette
* Brussel sprout leaves, smoked chicken; oyster mushroom in Wild Flower Vinaigrette.

Enjoy!

Bernard C. Casavant
Executive Chef
Chateau Whistler Resort

Fondue Time Among Friends
Cheese Fondue Savoyarde

The word 'fondue' comes from the french 'fondre' which means 'to melt', accurately describing a melting pot of 'Cheese Fondue'.

The French Alps & Switzerland produce great melting cheeses to accomodate this simple meal.

The fondue is the centerpiece of your party & builds a sociable & relaxed atmosphere, the fact of eating out of the sauce pot helps enhance friendship & relaxation.

Equiptment:
   A burner fueled with alcohol
   An enameled cast iron pot (le creuset)
   A set of long handled forks.

300 g. each Gruyère & Emmentaler cheese
1 clove garlic
1 shot Kirsch
½ litre dry white wine
2 tsp. cornstarch
   pinch each salt, nutmeg & white pepper

cont.

68

cont.

Grate the cheeses. Rub the fondue pot with the garlic. Combine the cheese & wine in the pot & stir over medium heat until smooth. Season to taste. Mix the cornstarch with the kirsch & add to fondue. Heat for 5 min. without allowing to bubble.

Serve with cubed french baguette. The fondue is best enjoyed with a cool, dry white wine.

As your guests enjoy, & the amount of cheese is diminishing in the pot, a gold crust of cheese will be forming on the bottom of the pot. This is called 'La Religieuse', the Nun & you must scrape it with your fork as it is the 'best part' of the meal!

After dinner a small shot of kirsch is a must. And don't forget the rules of fondue, when a man loses his bread, he must buy another bottle of wine, if a woman loses hers, she must kiss all the men at the table!

Bon Appetit! Joël   Chez Joël

Salmon Tarragon

4 salmon steaks
1 green pepper – cut in rings
1 red onion – cut in rings
1 lemon – cut in slices
1 c. medium dry white wine
   butter, tarragon, cornstarch
   tin foil

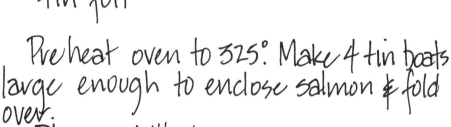

Preheat oven to 325°. Make 4 tin boats large enough to enclose salmon & fold over.

Place a little butter in each. Layer lemon, onion & pepper. Place salmon over & top with more lemon, onion & pepper. Sprinkle with tarragon. Pour about 2oz. wine over, close tin foil & bake 20 min.

Pour liquid into a saucepan & add a little more wine. Thicken sauce. Pour into each boat & bake another 10 min.

Remove from boats, garnish with grapes & serve with wild rice & steamed fresh vegetables. Serves 4.

Christine Ingrey

'Tired of Turkey' Pie

1 pie crust
2 c. turkey - chopped
1 c. celery - chopped
½ c. onion - chopped
½ c. whole cranberry sauce
   salt & freshly ground pepper
2 c. (or more) leftover vegetables -
   mashed. Yams & carrots are great.
½ eggs - beaten
½ c. milk
   salt & pepper, tarragon, dill & poultry
   seasoning to taste.

Prepare pie crust & place in pie plate.
Combine turkey, celery, onion & cranberries.
Season with salt & pepper. Put in pie crust.
   Combine mashed vegetables, eggs, milk
& seasonings to taste. Spread over first
mixture. Bake at 350° for 30-45 min.
Serve with a large green salad & dry white
wine.
   If you are tired of turkey, try this! ...
Otherwise store in freezer.

Carol Simmie

Dave's Creekhouse Chops

6-8 pork chops
2 medium onions - chopped
½ tsp. each cayenne & black pepper
1 tsp. each salt & paprika
2 tbsp. sugar
3 tbsp. cidar vinegar
4 tbsp. each ketchup & worchestershire
¾ c. water
30 oz. tomato juice

Place chops in a large flat baking dish. Combine all ingredients in a bowl. Pour this mixture over the chops & bake uncovered at 375° for 1½ - 2 hrs. or till done & the sauce is thick.

This sauce works well with ribs, chicken & cubed steak.

Serve with fresh vegetables in season. Serves 6-8.

Dave Asher
The Creekhouse

Enchiladas Del-Norte

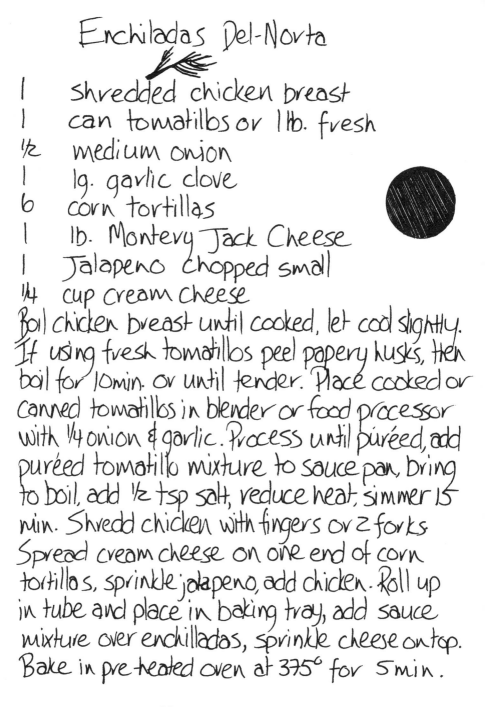

1	shredded chicken breast
1	can tomatillos or 1 lb. fresh
½	medium onion
1	lg. garlic clove
6	corn tortillas
1	lb. Montery Jack Cheese
1	Jalapeno chopped small
¼	cup cream cheese

Boil chicken breast until cooked, let cool slightly. If using fresh tomatillos peel papery husks, then boil for 10min. or until tender. Place cooked or canned tomatillos in blender or food processor with ¼ onion & garlic. Process until puréed, add puréed tomatillo mixture to sauce pan, bring to boil, add ½ tsp salt, reduce heat, simmer 15 min. Shredd chicken with fingers or 2 forks Spread cream cheese on one end of corn tortillas, sprinkle jalapeno, add chicken. Roll up in tube and place in baking tray, add sauce mixture over enchilladas, sprinkle cheese on top. Bake in pre-heated oven at 375° for 5 min.

Glen Tilley & friends
Border Cantina

Curry Prawns with Coconut

1½ lbs. prawns - shelled
2 tbsp. butter
1 tin each cream of mushroom & shrimp soup
¾ c. sour cream
1½ tsp. curry powder
2 tbsp. parsly chopped
  rice or pastry shells
  large flake coconut
  fresh black grapes

Melt butter in saucepan & add both soups. Stir until thoroughly blended. Stir in cream, curry powder & parsley. Heat. Add prawns & simmer 3 min. Don't overcook!
Serve over rice or pastry shells. Garnish with large flake coconut & fresh black grapes. Serves 4-6

The Whistler Seafood Corp.

74

Sea to Sky Seafood Lasagne

8 lasagne noodles - al dente 18 min.
2 tbsp. butter
1 c. onion chopped
1 8oz. pkg. cream cheese
1½ c. cottage cheese
1 egg - beaten
1 tsp. ea. sweet basil & tarragon
½ tsp. ea. salt & freshly ground pepper
2 10oz. tins mushroom soup
⅓ c. milk
⅓ c. dry white wine
½ lb. ea. crab, shrimp & scallops
4 c. Parmesan
½ c. aged cheddar - grated

Sauté onions in butter, add cheeses, egg & seasonings. Combine, in a bowl. soup, milk, & wine. Add seafood. Layer noodles, cheese mixture & seafood mixture. Repeat layers. Sprinkle with Parmesan & bake at 350° for 45 min. Top with cheddar & more basil. Melt under broiler. Let stand 15 min before serving. Serve with a green salad. Serves 8

Sonya McCarthy

75

Renée's Luxembourg Sweet Purple Cabbage

4-6 slices bacon - diced
1 medium onion-chopped
1 medium purple cabbage - shredded
2 apples - cored & diced
$\frac{1}{3}$ c. each cidar vinegar & water
$\frac{1}{4}$ c. brown sugar (to taste)
2-3 Bay leaves & fresh ground pepper

In a large pot saute' bacon & onions.
Add cabbage & saute. Add apples, vinegar
water, sugar & seasonings. Cover & simmer
30 min. Serve with roast pork & ...

Luxembourg Potato Pancakes

2-3 large potatoes, grated (raw)
1 medium onion - diced
Salt, pepper, nutmeg & fresh parsley to taste.
2 egg yolks - slightly beaten
2 egg whites - stiffly beaten.

Mix onion & potatoes, add enough flour to
bind. Mix, add remaining ingredients except
egg whites, which are folded in last. Saute.

Renee Titterton

Pork with Avgolemono Sauce

2 lb. celery - sliced
2 lb. lean pork
2 medium onions - chopped
½ c. butter
1 c. tomato sauce
salt & freshly ground black pepper - to taste
2 tbsp. flour
juice of 2 lemons
5 eggs - beaten

Simmer celery 10 min. Drain & reserve stock. Cut pork into 1" pieces & sauté with 2 tbsp. butter & the onion. Add tomato sauce & simmer 15 min. Add 1 c. or more of the stock, season with salt & pepper. Simmer until pork is tender. Drain & reserve liquid. Place pork & celery on platter.

Melt remaining butter & blend in flour, then reserved liquid. Simmer over low heat, stirring constantly, until thick.

Pour lemon juice slowly into eggs, beating constantly. Fold into sauce. Pour over pork & celery. Serves 4-6.

Peter at Peter's Underground

77

Chicken with Mustard & Lemon Sauce

4 chicken breasts
4 tbsp. olive oil
2 tsp. Dijon mustard
salt & freshly ground black pepper
1 clove garlic - slivered

Insert garlic under skin. Rub with oil & mustard. Season with salt & pepper. Grill on both sides for 10-15 min, baste.

1 tbsp. butter
1 small onion - finely chopped
1 tbsp. dry white wine
2 tbsp. chicken consommé
juice of ½ lemon
1 tbsp. Dijon mustard

Sauté onion in butter, add wine & consommé simmer over medium heat 2-3 min. Add lemon juice & Dijon, blend & reduce by simmering over medium heat 2-3 min. Season with salt & pepper. Pour sauce over chicken & serve. Serves 4.

The Managment & Staff
Trattoria di Umberto

Mahi Mahi with Bourbon Pecan Cream

1 lb. mahi mahi / or sea bass
2 tbsp. butter
1 shallot - minced
¼ c. dry Vermouth
1 oz. Jack Daniels
1 c. heavy cream
3 oz. pecan halves
1 papaya / or mango - chopped
fresh mint

Cut mahi mahi diagonally into 4 medallions. Season with salt, white pepper & lemon juice. Sauté in butter over low heat until medium rare, about 5 min. Remove from pan & discard most of butter. Sauté shallot & pecans lightly. Add vermouth & Jack Daniels, then cream. Reduce for 2 min. or until thickness covers the back of a spoon. Add papaya & return medallions. Simmer 2 min. Arrange on plate & pour sauce over. Garnish with fresh mint. Serve with wild rice. Serves 2.

Rolf Gunther
the Rim Rock Cafe & Oyster Bar
79

Chicken Florentyna

4 chicken breasts - boned, skinned, pounded to ¼"
  salt & freshly ground pepper
½ lb. fresh spinach - stemmed & steamed
¼ lb. mozzarella - cubed (4)
  flour, egg beaten with milk, breadcrumbs
3 tbsp. shallots - chopped
¼ c. fresh mushrooms - sliced
2 tbsp. butter
1 tsp. tarragon or 2 sprigs fresh tarragon
¼ c. dry white wine
½ c. heavy cream

Sprinkle chicken with salt & pepper. Place equal amounts of spinach & 1 piece of cheese on each breast. Wrap. Coat with flour, then milk & egg, & finish by coating with breadcrumbs. Bake at 425° for 15-20 min.

Sauté shallots & mushrooms in butter, add tarragon. Deglase pan with wine. Reduce by half, add cream & some freshly ground pepper. Pour over chicken breasts.

Serve with fresh vegetables in season or green salad. Serves 4.

Chef Ron Hozner / Florentynta's

80

Russel's Brussels

1 c. celery - sliced
1 medium onion - chopped
2 tbsp. butter
2 c. (or more!) brussel sprouts / halved
  white sauce
  salt & freshly ground white pepper
  nutmeg, garlic, oregano, basil & parsley.
½ lb. Ementhal cheese - diced
  breadcrumbs - sauteed
  slivered almonds

  Saute' celery & onions in butter. Parboil
brussels.
  Prepare a thick white sauce (the usual)
season to taste with salt & pepper, nutmeg,
garlic, oregano, basil & parsley. Melt
Ementhal in sauce.
  Fold ½ celery & onions, all of brussels into
sauce & place in a casserole. Top with the rest
of the celery & onions, breadcrumbs & lots
of slivered almonds. Bake ½ hr. at 350°.
Serve with any poultry. Serves 4-6.
  This recipe from the original Highland menu.

                              Russ Shepherd

Schwarzwald Torte

300 ml. hazelnuts
300 ml. powdered sugar
3-4 egg whites - whipped
1 - 250 ml. whipping cream
2 tsp. each vanilla & sugar
125 g. semi-sweet chocolate
1-2 tbsp. cocoa

Grind the nuts, mix with sugar & fold in egg whites (whipped to form stiff peaks) Divide into 5, spread thinly in a circle (approx. 8") on a cookie sheet.
Bake each in the middle of the oven @ 350°-375° for approx. 8-10 min. Cool.
Melt the chocolate & spread on wax paper on a flat surface. Cool. Cut into long thin triangles & rectangles.
Whip the cream with vanilla & sugar.
Assemble layers with whipped cream in between & on top. Decorate with the chocolate pieces, rectangles go on the sides & triangles on top. Sprinkle with cocoa.

Rose Marie Regitnig

82

Okanagan Pears in Red Wine

3 c. dry red wine
1 c. sugar
6 large Okanagan Pears
1 tsp. cinnamon
2 cloves
2 orange slices
2 lemon slices
1 c. whipping cream – whipped

Combine wine & sugar in glass or stainless steel bowl & stir until sugar dissolves. Set aside.

Peel & core pears, leaving stems attached, place in a pot just large enough to contain them. Add wine, cinnamon, cloves, orange & lemon slices.

Partly cover pot, bring to a boil & simmer on medium heat 15-20 min. Baste frequently. Cool.

Put pears on dessert plates, spoon wine mixture over them. Serve with whipped cream. Serves 6.

The Managment & Staff
Trattoria di Umberto
83

Doug's Pumpkin Cheesecake

1 graham wafer crust
1 250 g. pkg. cream cheese - softened
1 c. pumpkin puree
¾ c. brown sugar - packed
3 eggs - beaten
1½ tbsp. flour
1 tsp. cinnamon
½ tsp. nutmeg
½ tsp. vanilla

Prepare crust & set aside. Whip cream cheese until smooth & creamy then add all remaining ingredients. Whip until smooth & well blended. Save time - use a blender if you have one.

Heat filling at medium heat until mixture starts to thicken about 6-8 min. Stir constantly. Pour into pie shell & bake at 375° for 15 min. or until firm to the touch. Refrigerate until set.

Garnish with pecan halves & top with a little whipped cream.

Doug at the Longhorn

Alta Vista Chalet Apricot Torte

5 tbsp. butter
½ c. sugar
5 egg yolks
2 squares chocolate - semi sweet - melted
5 egg whites
¾ c. flour
½ c. slivered almonds
2 tbsp. apricot jam
2 squares chocolate - semi sweet - melted

Preheat oven to 350°. Cream butter, sugar & egg yolks. Add melted chocolate. Fold in stiffly beaten egg whites. Then fold in flour mixed with almonds.

Pour into a greased & floured spring form pan. Bake 45-60 min.

When torte is cool spread with a very thin layer of apricot jam.

Melt semi-sweet chocolate & pour over.

Georgie Koffman
Alta Vista Chalet

85

Bananas Flambé & Ice Cream

¼ c. butter
2 bananas (firm), halved lengthwise
¼ c. brown sugar
½ tsp. cinnamon
¼ c. light rum
vanilla ice cream

In a small chafing dish melt butter, add bananas & sauté over medium heat until lightly browned. Turn over & sprinkle with brown sugar & cinnamon. Sauté until almost tender – this should all take under 5 min.

Lower heat, add rum & ignite – stand back!

Serve immediatly with vanilla ice cream.

Chef Warren Grommada
Araxis

86

Snow Angel's Pie

3 egg whites
¾ tsp. cream of tarter
¾ c. sugar

Beat egg whites until frothy, add cream of tarter. Gradually add sugar & beat till stiff. Spread on bottom & sides of a greased pie plate. Bake at 275° for 60 min. Set aside to cool.

½ c. sugar
1 tbsp. lemon peel
3 tbsp. lemon juice
3 egg yolks

Mix together & heat slowly over low heat, stirring constantly until thickened. Set aside to cool.

1 c. whipping cream - whipped

Fold filling into whipped cream & gently spoon into crust. Refrigerate overnight, or while skiing ... or while waiting for the snow angel!

Dorothy Sabey
Maddison's

Frozen Nougat, Frangelico Parfait

Ingredients #1:
4	Whole Eggs
1	Egg Yolk
150g.	Sugar

Ingredients #2:
75 mgs.	Dark nougat (hazelnut paste), melted
25 mgs.	Frangelico liqueur

Ingredient #3:
½ litre Whipping cream - whipped to soft peak stage.

Combine all items of #1, cook over heat as per sabayon technique. Add all items of #2, fold in carefully. Once the mixture has cooled, carefully fold in the whipping cream. Keep cold until ready to pour into the molds or glasses. Once in desired molds, freeze until solid.

cont.

cont.
Optional Presentations:

A. Plate Presentation:
Place unmolded parfait onto plate, decorate with chocolate swirls and pour fruit coulis on the side. As the final touch, you can decorate it with mint leaves or edible flowers.

B. Glass Presentation:
Pull out frozen parfaits in glasses just before serving time; decorate with a rosette of whipcream. Sprinkle fresh roasted hazelnuts over rosette and mint leaf as a final garnish.

Makes 12 servings

Good luck!

Bernard C. Casavant   Christian Mitzel
Executive Chef   Pastry Chef
       Chateau Whistler Resort

Cheesecake with Fresh Fruit

1 graham cracker crust

While crust is baking mix the following in blender:

1/4 c. sugar
2 eggs
1 large pkg. cream cheese - softened
3/4 c. any fresh fruit in season

Pour into slightly cooled crust. Bake at 350° for 20 min. While baking mix the following in blender:

1/4 c. sugar
1/2 tsp. vanilla
250 ml. sour cream
1/4 c. Triple Sec or...

Pour over slightly cooled cheescake & bake 10 min. Cool, then chill 2 hrs. Top with fresh fruit. Serves 6.

Cindy Carlson

Easy St. Chocolate Rum Mousse

1 c. chocolate chips
3 tbsp. hot, strong coffee
2 tbsp. dark rum
½ c. light cream, scalded
2 medium eggs
   whipped cream

Put all ingredients, except whipped cream into blender container. Blend at high speed for 2 min.
Pour into dessert glasses. Chill. Top with whipped cream & sprinkle with shaved chocolate. Serves 4.

Barbara Conrad

Mountain Blueberries & Zabaglione

6 egg yolks
2/3 c. sweet Marsala wine
4 tbsp. dry white wine
2 tbsp. sugar
fresh mountain blueberries or...
any fresh fruit in season

Put egg yolks, Marsala & white wine & sugar in stainless steel bowl. Set bowl in a pot of boiling water.

Slightly tip bowl towards you & beat with a thin wire whisk in a backward & forward motion.

Whisk constantly until egg yolks become light & thicken slightly. Be careful not to cook the eggs too fast as they will scramble.

Put fresh berries or fruit in the bottom of sherbet glasses. Pour zabaglione over & serve hot or cold. Serves 4.

The Managment & Staff
Trattoria di Umberto.

Note: all ingredients must be at room temperature.

Baker's Cottage Chocolate Pecan Pie

3 eggs - slightly beaten
1 c. light or dark corn syrup
1 pkg. (4 oz.) semi-sweet chocolate - melted & cooled
⅓ c. sugar
2 tbsp. butter - melted
1 tsp. vanilla
1½ c. pecan halves
1 9" pastry shell - unbaked

In a large bowl, mix eggs, corn syrup, chocolate, sugar, butter & vanilla until well blended. Fold in pecans. Pour into the pastry shell.

Bake at 350° for 50-60 min. or until knife inserted halfway between centre & edges comes clean. Cool on a wire rack.

Serve with whipped cream & chocolate shavings. Very rich! Serves 8.

Baker's Cottage

93

Orange Tofu Mousse

1 tbsp. unflavoured gelatin
¼ c. water
12 oz. very fresh tofu
2 egg yolks
¾ c. honey
¼ tsp. salt
6 oz. frozen orange juice concentrate
2 egg whites - stiffly whipped
   Orange slices & large flake coconut

Combine gelatin & water in small pot, heat until melted, stirring constanltly.

Blend tofu in blender until very smooth. Add egg yolks, honey & salt. Blend well. Add gelatin. Blend well. Add juice concentrate & blend well.

Pour into a bowl & fold egg whites in gently. Then pour into individual dessert glasses. Chill overnight. Garnish with orange slice & coconut. Serves 6.

Nada Minunzi

This recipe works well with raspberry, lemon & lime frozen juice concentrate.

94

White & Dark Chocolate Mousse Pie

500 ml. Oreo Cookies, crushed (no cream)
250 ml. clarified Butter
   Mix & press into form, bottom & sides. Refrigerate

Dark Chocolate Mousse:

150g. semi.sweet chocolate
3 egg yolks
25 ml. sugar
250 ml. whipping cream, whipped
   Melt chocolate in double boiler. Cream egg
yolks & sugar, stir into chocolate. Fold in
whipped cream. Pour into shell & refrigerate

White Chocolate Mousse:

150g. white chocolate
3 egg yolks
25 ml. sugar
250 ml. whipping cream, whipped.
   Repeat above procedure. Pour over dark
chocolate. Refrigerate.
   Sauce: Shave 100g. semi sweet chocolate
into 100 ml. whipping cream. Heat & pour over.

Chef Don Atkinson
Planters at the International Lodge
95

Alsation Pears

2 c. dry white wine
1½ c. sugar
juice of 2 lemons
1 c. water
6 pears - D'Anjou the best!
2 10 oz. pkg. frozen raspberries, thawed
2 tbsp. Grand Marnier
   whipped cream flavoured with Grand Marnier
   chocolate leaves

Frost 6 long stemmed glasses.
In a large pot put wine, water, 1 cup sugar, juice of 1 lemon & simmer gently, covered. Peel pears, being sure to leave the stem intact. Take a slice off the bottom of each so they will stand. Simmer the pears in the syrup for about 30 min. Remove from heat, cool, & then drain.

In blender puree raspberries, juice of 1 lemon, ½ c. sugar & Grand Marnier. Place pears in glasses & drizzle sauce over. Add a dash of whipped cream to one side & decorate with chocolate leaves. Serves 6.

Trudy Gruetzke/Going Nuts
96

Molly's Sunshine Pie

1½ c. chocolate graham crumbs
¼ c. brown sugar
⅓ c. butter - melted
3 c. miniature marshmallows
1 tin sliced pineapple (& juice)
2 tbsp. lemon juice
⅔ c. pineapple yogurt
1 c. fresh strawberries, sliced
1 c. whipping cream - whipped
1 banana - chopped

Combine graham crumbs, sugar & butter, press into a pie plate. Bake 8 min. at 375°.

Combine marshmallows, pineapple juice & lemon juice, heat until melted. Chill till thickened. Stir in yogurt. Chill. Fold in whipped cream & bananas. Layer this mixture with pineapple & strawberries in cooled crust.

Top with pineapple slice & strawberries, artfully arranged.

Molly Boyd

Citta's Pecan Pie

6 tbsp. butter
3 tbsp. vegetable shortening
2 c. flour with a pinch of salt
¼ c. water
5 medium eggs - beaten
¼ c. brown sugar
¾ c. corn syrup
1 tbsp. ea. molasses & vanilla
  pinch of nutmeg & cinnamon
¾ c. pecan halves.

Pastry: Cut butter & shortening into flour with a pastry knife or fingertips to make a course meal (abt. pea size). Slowly add water till dough just holds together. Relax in a bowl, (the dough, not you!) for 20 min. Roll out on a floured surface & place in a greased pie plate.

Filling: Combine remaining ingredients except pecans. Pour into pie shell & place pecans on top. Bake at 375° for 35 min. Cool. May be topped with whipped cream. Serves 8.

Citta's

98

Citta Coffee

½ oz. Baileys
½ oz. Kahlúa
1 oz. B & B

Pour liqueurs into a coffee glass, fill with hot, strong coffee. Top with whipped cream.

Hoz's Coffee

1 oz. Sambuca Nigra
1 oz. Carolan's Irish Cream

Pour liqueurs into a heated coffee glass or brandy snifter. Fill with strong, black coffee. Top with whipped cream & grated chocolate.

Longhorn Royal Flush

½ oz. Grand Marnier
½ oz. Amaretto
½ oz. Cointreau

Pour liqueurs into a heated brandy snifter. Fill with boiling water. Garnish with a slice of orange.

Parker's Paralizer

3/4 oz.   151 proof Barcardi Rum
3/4 oz.   Kahlua.

Top with coke & milk. Build over rocks
in a sling glass.

Jimmy D's

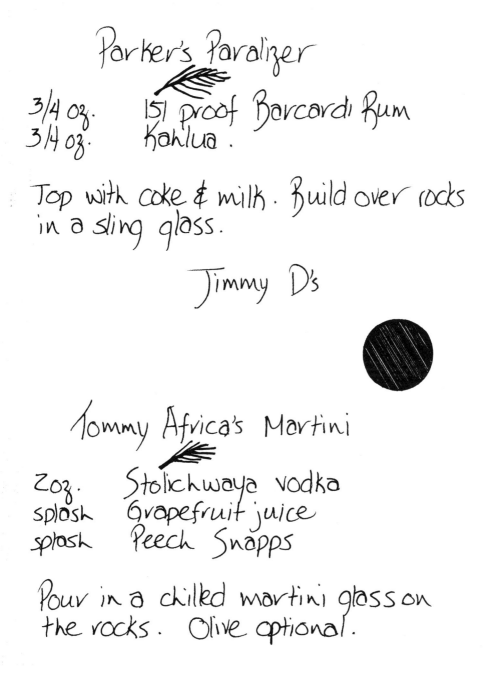

Tommy Africa's Martini

2 oz.   Stolichwaya vodka
splash   Grapefruit juice
splash   Peech Snapps

Pour in a chilled martini glass on
the rocks. Olive optional.

Bart's Place Bamm Bamm

3/4 oz. Baileys
3/4 oz. Amaretto
   Sugar the rim of a coffee glass. Pour in liqueurs, fill with hot, strong coffee, & top with whipped cream & a cherry.

Black Forest Coffee

3/4 oz. Kirsch-wasser
3/4 oz. Grand Marnier
   Sugar the rim of a coffee glass. Pour in liqueurs, fill with good, strong coffee & top with whipped cream & chocolate shavings.

Latte Chez Joël

1 oz. Benedictine
1/2 oz. Frangelico
3 oz. Steamed Milk
   Pour the steamed milk into a coffee glass. Layer liqueurs over milk. (Pour over a spoon) Top with foam from the steamed milk & chocolate powder.

Café Latte Joël

3 oz. steamed milk
2 oz. expresso coffee
¾ oz. Frangelico
¾ oz. Amaretto
Pour steamed milk into a coffee glass, then expresso. Layer liqueurs over. (Pour over a spoon.) Top with foam from the steamed milk & chocolate powder.

Tapley's Junior

½ oz. Tia Maria
½ oz. Triple Sec
2 oz. Baileys
Pour liqueurs into a coffee glass. Fill with hot, strong coffee. Top with whipped cream. Great over ice too.

Rim Rock Roll

3 oz. each hot chocolate & 3 oz. coffee
¾ oz. Kahlua
¾ oz. dark rum
Pour hot chocolate & coffee into a coffee glass. Add liqueurs, top with whipped cream & shavings.

102

Hans & Andi's Red Balloon

Put 1 scoop vanilla ice cream in frosted burgundy glass.

Blend 1 scoop strawberry ice cream & some cherry brandy. Add some whipping cream & blend at low spead till creamy.

Pour over the vanilla ice cream & decorate with whipping cream rosette & chocolate flakes.

Try with other kinds of liqueurs & ice creams. Baileys with coffee ice cream is good.

Raspberry Desire

1 pt. vanilla ice cream
1 pkg. frozen raspberries in syrup
3 oz. raspberry schnapps
3 oz. white rum

Blend until smooth, in the blender. Serve in long stemmed, frosted glasses. L. Hudson
Serves 6 - or more.

Barry T's Big O!

3/4 oz. Peppermint schnapps
1/4 oz. cream

Layer over spoon into shooter glass.

Club 10 Tony's 10 Dream

1 oz. Malibu Rum
½ oz. Peach Schnapps
2 oz. Pineapple juice
1 oz. Orange juice
   Mix in blender, garnish with orange slice & a cherry.

Floventyna's Licorice Nut

½ oz. Frangelico
½ oz. Sambuca
   ice
   Pour liqueurs over ice, stir. Strain into liqueur or sherry glass. Enjoy!

Planters Lounge Highland Martini

2 oz. vodka
dash dry vermouth
¼ oz. Drambuie
   ice
   Combine vodka & ice cubes in a shaker glass. Shake, add vermouth. Shake. Strain into martini glass, finish with Drambuie & a lemon twist.

Cuz's Strawberry Melon Marguirita

4 oz. Tequila
2 oz. Melon liqueur
1 c. frozen strawberries
5 oz. frozen lime juice
   Pour all ingredients into blender, fill with ice. Blend until ice is crushed. Serve in salted glasses. Serves 6. Buffalo Bills

Banana Nectar

¼ oz. Banana liqueur
¾ oz. Apricot brandy
3 oz. orange juice
2 oz. ginger ale
   Blend in blender. Pour over ice in a 12oz. glass. Garnish with a pineapple slice. T. Yonker

Barry T.'s Shannon Shooter

⅓ oz. Kaluha
⅓ oz. Dubonnet
⅓ oz. Brandy
   Layer over a spoon into shooter glass.

Rum Cream Liqueur

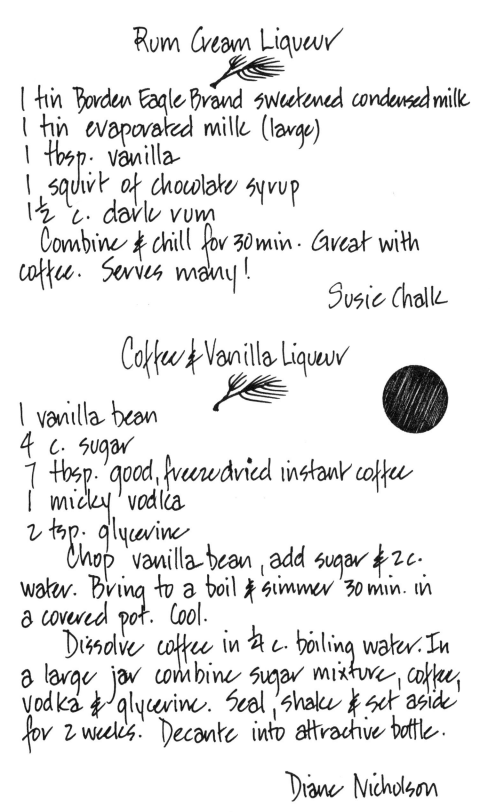

1 tin Borden Eagle Brand sweetened condensed milk
1 tin evaporated milk (large)
1 tbsp. vanilla
1 squirt of chocolate syrup
1½ c. dark rum

Combine & chill for 30 min. Great with coffee. Serves many!

Susie Chalk

Coffee & Vanilla Liqueur

1 vanilla bean
4 c. sugar
7 tbsp. good, freeze-dried instant coffee
1 mickey vodka
2 tsp. glycerine

Chop vanilla bean, add sugar & 2 c. water. Bring to a boil & simmer 30 min. in a covered pot. Cool.

Dissolve coffee in ½ c. boiling water. In a large jar combine sugar mixture, coffee, vodka & glycerine. Seal, shake & set aside for 2 weeks. Decante into attractive bottle.

Diane Nicholson

Chocolate Chip Cookie Chalet

Set aside 3 egg whites at room temperature for later use.

Cut cardboard patterns for 2 A-frame chalets. 1 Rectangle 4"x6", 1 Triangle Base 3½" Sides 5½".

Prepare a double batch of your favorite chocolate chip recipe & spread evenly on a 12"x18" cookie sheet (filling the corners) Bake as directed.

Take from oven & immediately place cardboard patterns on top & carve 4 rectangles, (sides/roof) & 4 triangles, don't forget the doors. (for 2 A-frame chalets)

Cut the remaining cookie mixture into bite size pieces, share amongst the cook & helpers! Let the A-frame parts cool.

Snow: (to assemble & decorate your chalet)

In a large bowl, beat the 3 egg whites with ¼ tsp. cream of tartar & 1 tsp. vanilla until foamy white & double in volume.

Beat in several cups of sifted icing sugar until the snow stands in peaks & holds a line when cut through with a knife.

Cont.

Cont.

Assemble your A-frame chalet using snow icing to stick it all together. (a cake decorating tool makes the job easy)

Spoon snow on top, make great gobs of snow & dripping 'icicles' from the sides.

Now the fun part – put colourful candies in the snow, decorating with abandon!

For special people, hide a small gift inside, don't forget to leave the door open so they can find it.

← more snow

lots & lots of snow →

← nougats & licorice chimney

draw snow shingles ➚

←smarties

licorice fence posts ↓

←allsorts

leave door open!

↑ lots of snow

more snow here

Today an A-frame, tomorrow a castle!

Isobel MacLaurin

108

Herschell's Favorite Carrot Cake

1 c. vegetable oil
4 large eggs
2 c. brown sugar
1 tbsp. cinnamon
2 c. carrots - grated
¾ c. pineapple pieces - drained
1 c. raisins
½ c. ea. walnuts/pecans & coconut
1½ c. ea. white flour & whole wheat flour
1 tbsp. baking soda & a pinch of salt

Cream oil, eggs, sugar & cinnamon. Add carrots, pineapple, raisins, nuts & coconut. Blend. Add flours, baking soda & salt. Blend. Should be a pretty gooey mix! Pour into a greased & lined 9" pan. Bake at 350° for about 1 hr.
   Cool & cover with 'Olga's Cream Cheese Icing' & chopped nuts.

Olga
The Southside Deli

109

Olga's Cream Cheese Icing

8 oz. cream cheese, softened
8 oz. butter - softened
  Beat like hell! Add:
2 c. icing sugar
2 tsp. vanilla
1 tsp. lemon rind or 1 tbsp. lemon juice
  Beat like hell again! Spread over
'Herschell's Favorite Carrot Cake' & spinkle
with chopped nuts.

                              Olga
          The Southside Deli

Whistler Valley Trail Mix

1 lb. Spanish peanuts - skins on
½ lb. Sunflower seeds - hulled
¼ lb. Whole almonds - skins on
¼ lb. Cashew pieces
¼ lb. Pumpkin seeds
¼ lb. Banana chips
¼ lb. each Dried Apricots & Pears - sliced
1 handful each Black currants, yogurt
  raisins & chia seeds.
  Mix & store in a cool place. This will
get you where you're going!

Skier's Spicy Zucchini Bread

2 c. flour
½ tsp. baking soda
1 tsp. cinnamon
½ tsp. allspice
1 tsp. baking powder
½ tsp. salt
½ c. chopped nuts & or raisins
2 eggs
⅔ c. vegetable oil
⅔ c. white sugar
⅓ c. brown sugar
½ tsp. vanilla
2 c. unpeeled zucchini - grated

In dedication to Pat, who spurred David on to Bigger & Better things!

Mix flour, baking soda, cinnamon, allspice, baking powder, salt & chopped nuts & or raisins in a bowl.

In another bowl beat together eggs, oil, sugars. Add vanilla & zucchini, mix. Combine wet & dry ingredients & mix well.

Pour into a greased & floured 9"x5" loaf pan. Bake at 350° for 55-60 min.

Chef David Small/Blackcomb Mt.

111

Coconut Carrot Cookies

1 c. carrots - cooked & mashed
¾ c. sugar
1 c. butter - softened
2 eggs
2 c. flour
2 tsp. baking powder
½ tsp. salt
¾ c. shredded or flaked coconut

Pre heat oven to 400°. Cream together carrots, sugar, butter & eggs. Combine dry ingredients & mix well with carrot mixture.
Drop by teaspoonfuls 2" apart on to ungreased cookie sheet. Bake 10-12 min. Cool & frost with:

3 c. icing sugar - sifted
⅓ c. butter - softened
2-3 tbsp. orange juice concentrate
2 tsp. grated orange rind

Cream together icing sugar & butter. Add orange juice & rind. Mix.

Bridget Strobl

Rob's Pumpkin Muffins

¾ c. bran
¾ c. whole wheat flour
¾ c. brown sugar
1½ tsp. cinnamon
1 tsp. baking powder
1 tsp. baking soda
1 c. raisins
1 c. pumpkin - pureed
2 eggs - beaten
½ c. sunflower oil
½ c. yogurt or buttermilk

Mix all dry ingredients & raisins.
Add pumpkin, eggs, oil, & yogurt or
buttermilk. Mix thoroughly
Fill muffin tins ¾ full. Bake at
350° for 10-12 min.
Cool & put in your backpack for
mid afternoon skiing munchies!

Rob Boyd.

113

Utralight Peanut Butter Chocolate Chip Cookies

1 c. peanut butter
1 c. butter / softened
½ c. white sugar
¾ c. brown sugar
2 eggs
2½ c. flour
1 tsp. baking powder
1 c. semi sweet chocolate chips
2 c. puffed wheat
  milk

Pre heat oven to 350°. Beat peanut butter & butter till smooth, gradually add sugars & beat until fluffy. Add eggs, one at a time & beat. Mix flour & baking powder & blend in. Add chocolate chips & mix. Mix puffed wheat in (with hands). Add enough milk to hold dough together.

Roll into balls, place on a greased cookie sheet & press with a fork. Bake 10 min. or until golden. Careful - do not overbake.

The 7 Day Wonder

Mountain Muffins

4½ c. whole wheat flour
3 tsp. baking powder
3 tsp. baking soda
¾ tsp. salt
3 tsp. cinnamon
½ c. brown sugar
    Mix all dry ingredients in a bowl.

1½ c. vegetable oil
1 c. blackstrap molasses
1 30oz. tin unsweetened crushed pineapple
3 eggs – beaten
1½ tsp. vanilla
    Mix all moist ingredients in a bowl.
Blend together dry & moist ingredients. Add:

1 c. bran & 1 c. oats
    Mix in thoroughly. Add at this time a
handful of each, raisins, walnuts, sunflower
seeds, berries or...
    Batter should be very moist, almost runny..
    Bake at 350° for 30 min. Makes 3 doz.

Tricia Marshall
The Cake Lady

115

World Cup Granola Bars

1½ c. butter - softened
1¼ c. brown sugar
1 egg
¼ c. molasses
½ orange (rind & all) - puree'
1¾ c. whole wheat flour
1 tsp. baking soda
1½ c. rolled oats
1 c. coconut
1 c. raisins
½ c. nuts or sesame seeds or...

Cream together butter, sugar, egg, molasses & orange. Combine all dry ingredients & mix thoroughly with butter etc.

Press into large flat pan & Bake 10 min. at 350° or until browned.

Cut while warm, but cool before removing from pan. Dig in! We all did, at the last World Cup race.

Rob Boyd

The Old Coolchouse Muffins

2 eggs - beaten
2/3 c. vegetable oil
2 c. ripe bananas - mashed
2 tsp. vanilla
2/3 c. white sugar
2/3 c. brown sugar
2 c. unbleached white flour
1 tsp. baking soda
2 tsp. baking powder
2 c. bran
2/3 c. each raisins & walnuts or...

Mix wet ingredients in a bowl, mix dry ingredients in another bowl. Combine & mix well. Fill lined muffin tins 2/3 full. Bake 25 min. at 425°.

Jan Systad
Husky Deli

This is Jan's original recipe from the Coolhouse. She often substituted applesauce, pumpkin or carrot purée for the bananas.

117

Whole Wheat Cakes with Cheese

1 c. butter - softened
2 c. aged cheddar - grated
   dash Tabasco
   dash Worcestershire
   pinch cayenne
1½ c. whole wheat flour
4 c. puffed wheat - crushed slightly
   salt
   milk

Cream together butter, cheese & seasonings. Mix in flour, puffed wheat & salt to taste. (Mix with hands - its easier) Add enough milk to hold dough together.
   Roll dough into 2 logs, wrap in wax paper & chill 1 hr.
   Preheat oven to 350°. Cut logs into ¼" rounds & place on a greased cookie sheet. Bake 10-12 min. Cool.
   Great hiking fare & great with home made soup. Like rice cakes but more interesting.

                    The 7 Day Wonder.

Dog W. A. G. Biscuits

1 c. white flour
1 c. whole wheat flour
½ c. wheat germ
½ c. powdered milk
½ tsp. salt
½ c. cheese - grated
6 tbsp. butter or bacon fat
1 egg
1 tsp. brown sugar

Mix flours, wheat germ, powdered milk, salt & cheese. If your dog likes nuts or seeds you may want to add a few now. Cut in butter or bacon fat. Beat together egg & brown sugar & add. Add enough water (approx ½ c.) to make a stiff dough.

Roll out on floured board & cut into shapes appealing to dogs!

Bake at 300° for 30 min., turn & bake an additional 30 min. or until dry & crunchy.

Dorothy Sabey

Please send me _____ copies @ $17.95 each
plus $2.00 handling charge within Canada.
Amount enclosed $_____ in Canadian funds.
Please Print:
Name: _____
Address: _____
City: _____
Province: _____
Postal Code: _____
Country: _____

Please send me _____ copies @ $17.95 each
plus $2.00 handling charge within Canada.
Amount enclosed $_____ in Canadian funds.
Please Print:
Name: _____
Address: _____
City: _____
Province: _____
Postal Code: _____
Country: _____

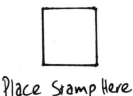

Whistler Weekend Cookbook
c/o Elsie Cumming
#304-2 Renaissance Sq.
New Westminster, B.C.
Canada
V3M 6K3

Whistler Weekend Cookbook
c/o Elsie Cumming
#304-2 Renaissance Sq.
New Westminster, B.C.
Canada
V3M 6K3